Introduction

France has a proud tradition of building its own cutting-edge combat aircraft – a tradition that is inextricably linked to one company: Dassault. Marcel Bloch had been a successful aircraft manufacturer before the Second World War, but when France was looking to rearm during the post-war period he seized the initiative to produce the first all-French jet fighter, the Ouragan.

From this starting point, Dassault kept pace with its rivals by rapidly evolving the Mystère series through numerous iterations during the 1950s. The company only truly hit its stride, however, with the outstanding and extraordinarily successful Mirage III series. The lightweight Mirage III with its delta wing and distinctive dart-like appearance offered outstanding performance and quickly became a combat-proven product – scoring kills against MiG-17s and MiG-21s in Israeli hands during the late 1960s.

It did well on the export market and even better when the French stripped out its costly and hard-to-maintain radar, calling the resulting simplified aircraft Mirage 5. This was then marketed as a cut-price multirole fighter and sold to smaller and more budget-conscious air forces.

Dassault's 'the customer is always right' attitude resulted in an astonishing wealth of different variants, many tailored to the specific needs of the purchaser in a way that other combat aircraft seldom were. And then there were the copies – Israel famously acquired the plans to the Mirage III and built its own version, known as the IAI Nesher. The Nesher then became the

Kfir, which is still availa[...]rly 65 years after the Mirage III first flew, and this in turn spawned the South African Atlas Cheetah.

Meanwhile, Dassault had supplied the highly capable Étendard IV and Super Étendard as carrier fighters for the French Navy and followed up the Mirage III/5's success with the Mirage F1. With a conventional non-delta layout, the F1 proved to be an excellent multirole fighter and again garnered numerous orders from international customers.

The French Air Force entered the modern era with the superb Mirage 2000 – yet another versatile combat aircraft which, despite looking remarkably similar to the Mirage III/5, was completely new and embodied all the latest technological advances in a compact and relatively affordable package.

Most recently, Dassault's excellent Rafale has been at the forefront of French military aviation and has recently enjoyed a remarkable degree of success in attracting international buyers. Now Dassault is working with German and Spanish partners on FCAS – Europe's Future Combat Air System – but its legacy fighters continue to fly and fight with air forces around the world.

This publication chronicles the combat jets of the French Air Force from 1952 to the present day through the beautiful artworks of renowned aviation illustrator JP Vieira. I hope you enjoy marvelling at the incredible variety of designs as much as I have.

Dan Sharp

ABOUT THE ARTIST

JP Vieira is an illustrator producing military history and aviation-themed artwork.

He is entirely self-taught and aims to constantly improve both his technical and digital methods. His attention to detail and constant pursuit of improvement makes his artworks both accurate and artistically pleasing.

JP has collaborated with numerous authors, editors and publishers on a wide variety of publications – including USAF Fighters, US Navy Jet Fighters, Marine Corps Jet Fighters and most recently US Jet Fighters in Foreign Service for Tempest Books.

Two Dassault Rafale M F2s of the Aéronavale over Iraq during Operation Inherent Resolve on January 8, 2016.

CONTENTS

034 | **DASSAULT MIRAGE III**

052 | **DASSAULT MIRAGE 5**

072 | **DASSAULT MIRAGE IV**

076 | **DASSAULT MIRAGE F1**

090 | **SEPECAT JAGUAR**

102 | **DASSAULT MIRAGE 2000**

116 | **DASSAULT RAFALE**

All illustrations:
JP VIEIRA

Design:
DRUCK MEDIA PVT. LTD.

Publisher:
STEVE O'HARA

Production editor:
DAN SHARP

Published by:
MORTONS MEDIA GROUP LTD, MEDIA CENTRE, MORTON WAY, HORNCASTLE, LINCOLNSHIRE LN9 6JR

Tel. 01507 529529

MORTONS MEDIA GROUP LTD

ISBN: 978-1-911703-08-2

DASSAULT
OURAGAN

DE SAXCE

Z-SS

1952-1990s

BB

Marcel Bloch was already a pivotal figure in the French aviation industry long before the Second World War – not just an engineer but an industrialist managing thousands of staff across multiple factory sites. So when France emerged from the war years and began to rebuild its armed forces, he was well placed to assemble the team and sign the deals needed to create the nation's first jet fighter: the Ouragan.

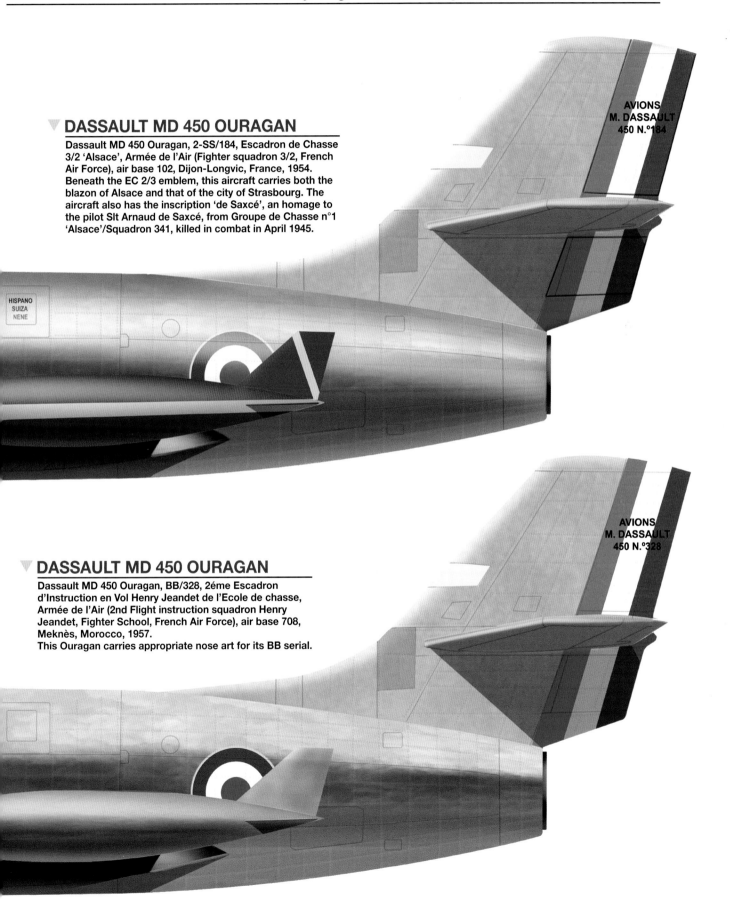

▽ DASSAULT MD 450 OURAGAN

Dassault MD 450 Ouragan, 2-SS/184, Escadron de Chasse 3/2 'Alsace', Armée de l'Air (Fighter squadron 3/2, French Air Force), air base 102, Dijon-Longvic, France, 1954. Beneath the EC 2/3 emblem, this aircraft carries both the blazon of Alsace and that of the city of Strasbourg. The aircraft also has the inscription 'de Saxcé', an homage to the pilot Slt Arnaud de Saxcé, from Groupe de Chasse n°1 'Alsace'/Squadron 341, killed in combat in April 1945.

HISPANO SUIZA NENE

AVIONS M. DASSAULT 450 N.°184

▽ DASSAULT MD 450 OURAGAN

Dassault MD 450 Ouragan, BB/328, 2éme Escadron d'Instruction en Vol Henry Jeandet de l'Ecole de chasse, Armée de l'Air (2nd Flight instruction squadron Henry Jeandet, Fighter School, French Air Force), air base 708, Meknès, Morocco, 1957.
This Ouragan carries appropriate nose art for its BB serial.

AVIONS M. DASSAULT 450 N.°328

DASSAULT MD 450 OURAGAN

Dassault MD 450 Ouragan, 155, Escadron de Chasse 3/4 'Flandre', SPA 160 'Diable Rouge', Armée de l'Air (Fighter squadron 3/4, Flight 160, French Air Force), Patrouille de France, air base 136, Bremgarten, West Germany, 1956. The famous Patrouille de France aerobatic team flew the Ouragan from 1954 until 1957; in the early years, the team was constituted with aircraft and personnel from several different units consecutively.

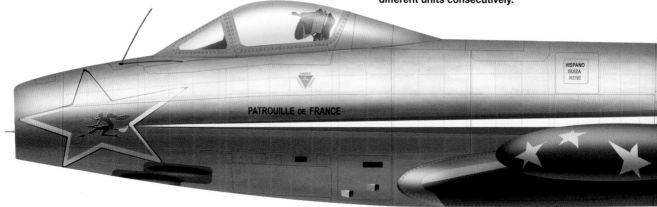

DASSAULT MD 450 TOOFANI

Dassault MD 450 Toofani, IC568, No. 29 Squadron 'Scorpions', Indian Air Force, Halwara Air Force Station, Punjab, India, 1958.
This squadron flew the Toofani (Indian designation for the Dassault Ouragan) for a few months in 1958, being disbanded after that; the squadron would re-form in 1967 flying the MiG-21.

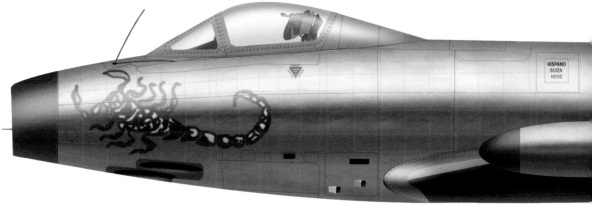

DASSAULT MD 450 TOOFANI

Dassault MD 450 Toofani, IC556, No. 47 Squadron 'Archers', Indian Air Force, Halwara Air Force Station, Punjab, India, 1965.
No. 47 Squadron flew the Toofani from 1959 until 1968, participating in the Indo-Pakistani War of 1965.

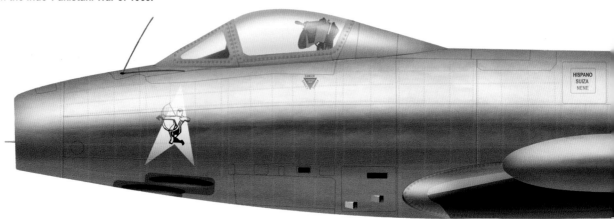

Released from Buchenwald concentration camp in April 1945, Marcel Bloch returned to France eager to re-enter the aircraft building industry. His company, Société Anonyme des Avions Marcel Bloch (SAAMB), still existed and he was able to reclaim and reorganise it – including his factories at Saint-Cloud, Boulogne and Talence. Many of his original skilled employees returned to him between May and November 1945.

The company was reorganised again in November with SAAMB becoming a holding company, leasing its factories to subsidiaries at the three sites. Construction work began on a light twin-prop transport aircraft, the MB 303 Flamant or 'Flamingo', for the French Air Force and while this was being built Bloch laid plans for something much more ambitious – France's first home grown jet fighter.

Bloch signalled his intent in January 1947 by changing both his own name and his company's name to Marcel Dassault. Famously, 'Dassault' had been the nom de guerre used by his elder brother Darius Paul Bloch as a member of the French resistance. The numerical sequence of Bloch types was continued but with 'MD' instead of 'MB'.

Initial designs for the new fighter, worked up by Dassault's engineers, were presented to the French government in September 1947 but did not result in an order. The company pressed on using its own funds however, and detailed design commenced that December. Construction of a single prototype began in April 1948 as the MD 450 and the government finally issued a contract for three prototypes on June 29, 1948.

A crucial aspect of the design, which otherwise leaned on contemporary American fighter layouts, particularly that of the F-84, was the engine. Fortunately, the French arm of Hispano-Suiza had begun to build the British Rolls-Royce Nene centrifugal flow turbojet under licence so it could be fitted to de Havilland Vampire fighters that were also being built under licence in France. As such Dassault was easily able to secure an initial supply from Rolls-Royce itself and to then source further examples from the local licence-builder.

The MD 450 Ouragan or 'Hurricane' was indeed rather similar to the F-84 Thunderjet in appearance, with low-set straight wings, a nose intake, full-vision teardrop canopy and tricycle undercarriage. It was smaller though, weighed about a ton less, and had thinner wings which were more like those of Lockheed's F-80 Shooting Star.

The first prototype, MD 450 01, made its flight debut on February 28, 1949, piloted by Kostia Rozanoff, and when it proved to be a success, the French government placed an order for 150 production model Ouragans.

And once the third prototype had been delivered, the French government ordered 15 pre-production test aircraft. Only a dozen of these would actually

▼ DASSAULT MD 450 OURAGAN

Dassault MD 450 Ouragan, 42, 113 squadron 'Hornet', Israel Defense Force/Air Force, Hatzor air base, Israel, 1956.
Besides the prominent shark mouth, this aircraft has the yellow and black identification stripes for its participation in the Suez conflict of 1956.

▼ DASSAULT MD 450 OURAGAN

Dassault MD 450 Ouragan, 64, 113 squadron 'Hornet', Israel Defense Force/Air Force, Hatzor air base, Israel, 1966.
Israeli Ouragans had a significant career and still participated in the 1967 Six-Day War.

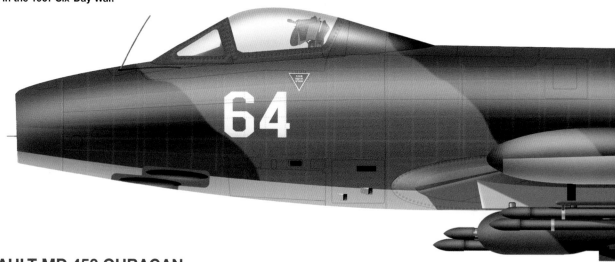

▼ DASSAULT MD 450 OURAGAN

Dassault MD 450 Ouragan, 704, Fuerza Aérea Salvadoreña (Salvadorean Air Force), El Salvador, 1982.
El Salvador acquired 18 Ouragans in the early 1970s from Israel; the aircraft would see action in the country's internal conflicts up until the early 1990s.

be built but they were used to trial a variety of engines, different weapons and payload arrangements and even a solid-nose radar installation with side intakes.

Deliveries of the first production model Ouragans commenced in 1952, with the type replacing the French Air Force's increasingly antiquated de Havilland Vampires. All examples had wingtip fuel tanks fitted. Armament was a quartet of Hispano Mark V 20mm cannon under its nose intake and a metric ton of stores could be carried under the type's wings. A typical load might include two 450kg bombs, or eight 105mm Matra T10 rockets and a pair of 460-litre napalm bombs, or just 16 rockets.

The first 50, designated MD 450A, had Rolls-Royce-made Nene 102 engines while later examples, designated MD 450B, had Hispano-Suiza-made Nene 104Bs. The latter engine was somewhat lighter than its predecessor and offered marginally improved thrust.

The Ouragan was reportedly a stable gun platform with good handling characteristics but suffered from an unfortunate tendency to enter a flat spin if the pilot attempted to pull a tight turn. The type was phased out of frontline service with the French Air Force starting in May 1955 as the somewhat better Mystère IV became available and the last French examples were retired from operational units in 1961. A handful would soldier on into the mid-1960s as advanced trainers. The Patrouille de France display team, having started out in 1953 with Republic F-84G Thunderjets, flew the Ouragan from 1954 to 1957 before switching to the Mystère IV.

A single Ouragan underwent modifications to make the type suitable for rough field operations in Algeria – brake parachutes were installed to decrease landing distance and their single-wheel undercarriage mainwheels were upgraded to two wheels per leg with low pressure tyres. The 'Barougan', as it was dubbed, first flew on February 24, 1954, with Paul Boudier at the controls. However, budget cuts meant it was never ordered into production.

Seventy-one Ouragans fitted with the improved Nene 105 engine were ordered by India in 1953 and most of them had been delivered by the end of the year. Another 33 were later bought from French Air Force stocks. In Indian service, the aircraft was given the name 'Toofani', the Hindi word for Hurricane, and it was retired from front line units starting in 1958.

The Israeli Air Force ordered 24 Mystère IICs in 1955 but when the type was found to have structural issues it bought 75 Ouragans instead as a stopgap while waiting for a delivery of the new Mystère IVA. Deliveries commenced just in time for the type to be used during Operation Musketeer in 1956 – the Israeli, British and French invasion of Egypt to secure the Suez Canal. Ouragans of the IAF flew close support missions and even successfully engaged Egyptian MiG-15s in air-to-air combat.

Before long the IAF's Ouragans were shifted to the advanced trainer role but they would see combat once again during the Six-Day War in 1967. Eighteen Israeli Ouragans were purchased by El Salvador in 1975, where they would continue to fly into the early 1990s.

DASSAULT MYSTÈRE IIC

The MD 452 Mystère II series was effectively Dassault's learning curve as the company struggled to develop its jet fighter into a modern and internationally competitive machine. The Mystère IIC was the variant that would enter series production.

1954–1963

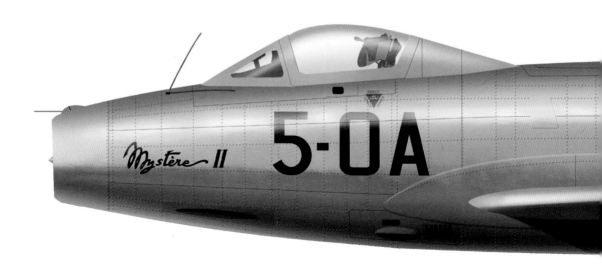

Jet fighter development rapidly became its own fiercely contested arms race during the 1950s and now, thanks to Dassault and the Ouragan, France was competing on the world stage with designs from the US, Britain and Soviet Union.

The Ouragan, with its straight wings, had been out of date even before it flew and Dassault quickly moved to advance its design by adding thinner 30-degree swept wings and modified tail surfaces. This sole prototype was designated MD 452 Mystère I 01 and made its first flight on February 23, 1951, with Kostia Rozanoff at the controls. Two further Mystère I prototypes were built featuring the latest Rolls-Royce turbojet design, made by Hispano-Suiza, the Tay 250.

Then two Tay-powered MD 452 Mystère IIA prototypes were made, each armed with four Hispano 20mm cannon, and one of them became the first French aircraft to hit Mach 1 – albeit

in a dive – on October 28, 1951. Four MD 452 Mystère IIB prototypes with the alternative armament of two 30mm DEFA cannon followed.

The MD 452 Mystère IIC differed in being designed to accommodate a single SNECMA Atar 101 axial-flow turbojet – the Rolls-Royce engines all having been of the centrifugal type. The Atar 101C had been developed by team of former BMW turbojet designers who had come to work for the French after the war and was based on their late-war P 3306 project.

Eleven pre-production Mystère IICs were made, nine of them with the Atar 101C and two with the experimental afterburning Atar 101F. The French Air Force ordered 150 production examples and these would be powered by Atar 101D engines

with armament of two 30mm DEFA cannon. They also had increased tail sweep and internal alterations to improve their fuel systems.

The first production Mystère IIC flew in June 1954 and was delivered four months later. In service, it was found that the Mystère IIC was prone to structural failure during high-speed flight and as such by the time the last Mystère IIC was delivered in 1957 the type had already left front line service and was being used as an advanced trainer. It was finally retired entirely in 1963 and there were no foreign customers.

The last French jet based on the Ouragan was the MD 453 Mystère III or Mystère de Nuit two-seat night fighter – which had a solid nose, side intakes, 32-degree wing sweepback and first flew on July 18, 1952, piloted by Rozanoff. Only one prototype was made and it eventually ended its flying career as a flying test-bed for SNCASO ejection seats.

AVIONS DASSAULT 452 N.°110

◀ DASSAULT MD 452 MYSTÈRE IIC

Dassault MD 452 Mystère IIC, 10-SB/110, Escadron de Chasse 3/10 'Aunis', Escadrille SPA 93 – Canard, Armée de l'Air (Fighter Squadron 3/10, Flight SPA 93, French Air Force), air base 110, Creil, France, 1956.
The first transonic French aircraft, the Mystère II did not attract any export orders and enjoyed only brief frontline service with French units.

AVIONS DASSAULT 452 N.° 16

▼ DASSAULT MD 452 MYSTÈRE IIC

Dassault MD 452 Mystère IIC, 5-OA/16, Escadron de Chasse 2/5 Île-de-France, Armée de l'Air (Fighter Squadron 2/ 5, French Air Force), air base 115, Orange-Caritat, France, 1957.
Mystères IICs were operated by EC 2/5 only for a year before being replaced by Mystère IVs.

DASSAULT
MYSTÈRE IVA

1953-1980s

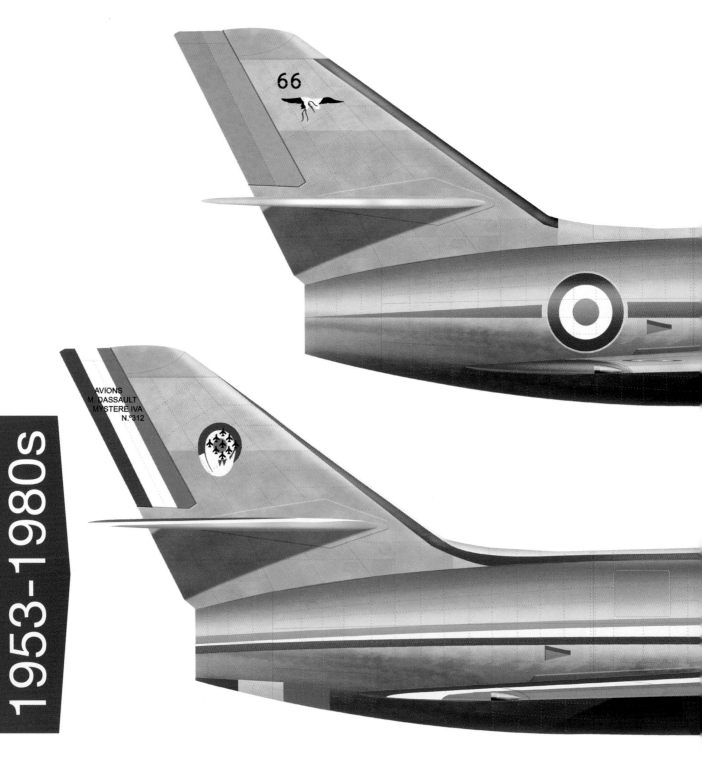

AVIONS
M. DASSAULT
MYSTÈRE IVA
N.°312

The Mystère IV featured a whole new airframe but still loosely retained the form of its slightly earlier namesakes. It was also capable of overmatching a MiG-15 in a way that the others couldn't.

H aving enjoyed success with the Ouragan and having effectively upgraded it into the Mystère II, Dassault rapidly took a full evolutionary step with the Mystère IV – introducing a new oval-section fuselage, thinner more swept-back wings and new tail surfaces. Just one prototype was made, Mystère IV 01, and it first flew on September 28, 1952, piloted by Kostia Rozanoff.

The French government was impressed when the aircraft proved capable of breaking the sound barrier in a dive and an order for 22 pre-production examples was placed in October. However, this was cancelled in December

and an order was placed for eight improved Mystère IVAs instead.

A US Air Force delegation including Charles 'Chuck' Yeager visited France that month to test French combat aircraft and this led to the United States purchasing 225 Mystère IVAs as a gift to the French Air Force on April 25, 1953.

The first production standard Mystère IVA made its flight debut on May 29, 1954, piloted by Paul Boudier, and was formally handed over to the American authorities on June 18, who then passed it on to the French Air Force.

The Mystère IVA entered service on May 25, 1955, and all 225 had been delivered by June 18, 1956.

A total of 411 Mystère IVAs were made – 114 of them fitted with the Rolls-Royce Tay and the remainder with the Hispano-Suiza Verdon 350, a more powerful Tay variant.

All Mystère IVAs had a pair of DEFA 30mm cannon and the ability to carry a combined total of up to 1,000kg of stores on four underwing pylons. This could include drop tanks, a variety of bombs or 68mm unguided SNEB rockets.

Israel expressed an early interest in the Mystère IVA but initially had to settle for Ouragans when the Mystère IIC proved to be an unattractive investment. It was eventually able to acquire 60 of

▼ DASSAULT MD 454 MYSTÈRE IVA

Dassault MD 454 Mystère IVA, 8-NX/66, Escadron de Chasse 2/8 'Nice', Escadrille SPA 73 'Cigogne japonaise', Armée de l'Air (Fighter Squadron 2/8, Flight SPA 73, French Air Force), air base 120, Cazaux, France, 1979. One of the oldest units of the French Air Force, SPA 73 flew the Mystère IV from 1964 until 1982, when it was replaced by the Alpha Jet.

▼ DASSAULT MD 454 MYSTÈRE IVA

Dassault MD 454 Mystère IVA, 312, Patrouille de France, Armée de l'Air (French Air Force), air base 133, Nancy-Ochey, France, 1961. The demonstration team flew the Dassault Mystère IVA from 1957 until 1964.

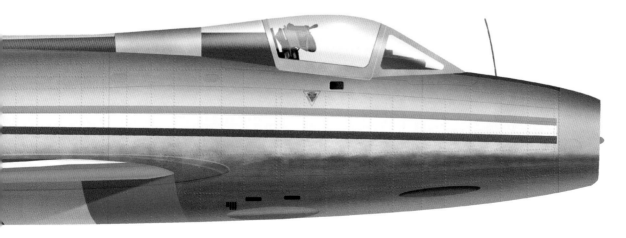

FRENCH COMBAT JETS | Dassault Mystère IVA

France's own Verdon-powered Mystère IVAs in 1956, with the first 24 arriving that April. These participated in Operation Musketeer in October 1956 alongside French Mystère IVAs and the type acquitted itself well against Egypt's MiG-15s. Israel's remaining 36 Mystère IVAs were delivered after the conflict. During the Six-Day War of 1967, the IAF was still able to field two full squadrons of Mystère IVAs.

In 1957, India received the first of 110 new-build Mystère IVAs it had ordered and these were used to fly close support missions during the Indo-Pakistani War of 1965. Also in 1957, the Mystère IVA was adopted by the Patrouille de France, replacing the display team's Ouragans,

before it was itself replaced in 1964 by the Fouga Magister.

The Mystère IVA would remain in frontline service with French units until the early 1960s and would continue in the ground-attack role until 1975. Even then, it would enjoy another five years' service as an operational trainer – finally being retired outright in 1982.

The Mystère IVA was swiftly developed into the IVB, which was almost a new aircraft again – with a new fuselage, new tailfin and radar gunsight. The first prototype, powered by a Rolls-Royce RA.7R Avon, first flew in December 1953. A second example flew in June 1954 and a third, powered by an Atar 101F, in March 1955. A series of seven pre-production Mystère IVBs were made, two with SEPR 66 rocket motors for additional thrust and two with the afterburning Atar 101 G-2. The Mystère IVB would subsequently serve as the basis for the Super Mystère.

A prototype Mystère IVN two-seat night fighter with a retractable rocket launcher in addition to its two 30mm DEFA cannon was built but the project went no further.

▼ DASSAULT MD 454 MYSTÈRE IVA

Dassault MD 454 Mystère IVA, IA-1017, No. 1 Squadron 'Tigers', Indian Air Force, Adampur Air Force Station, India, 1966.
No. 1 Squadron flew its Mystères during the 1965 war with Pakistan; this aircraft displays appropriately feline nose art and carries Matra T10 rockets.

▼ DASSAULT MD 454 MYSTÈRE IVA

Dassault MD 454 Mystère IVA, 63, 101 Squadron, Israel Defense Force/Air Force, Hatzor air base, Israel, 1956.
Israeli Mystères were used operationally in the Suez Crisis of 1956, shortly after their delivery from France; this aircraft is painted with the 'invasion stripes' used during that conflict.

DASSAULT
SUPER MYSTÈRE B2

▶ DASSAULT SUPER MYSTÈRE B2

Dassault Super Mystère B2, 10-RG/31, Escadron de Chasse 2/10 'Seine', Armée de l'Air (Fighter Squadron 2/10, French Air Force), 110 air base, Creil, France, 1967. The Super Mystère was operated by this unit for around 16 years until it was replaced, in 1974, by the Mirage IIIC.

▶ DASSAULT SUPER MYSTÈRE B2

Dassault Super Mystère B2, 12-YK/156, Escadron de Chasse 1/12, SPA 162 'Tigre', Armée de l'Air (Fighter Squadron 1/12, Flight 162, French Air Force), RAF Greenham Common, UK, 1977.
EC 1/12 sent this stripy Super Mystère to the NATO Tiger Meet of 1977.

Bearing a striking resemblance to the contemporary though somewhat larger Republic F-100 Super Sabre, the Super Mystère was the last of an illustrious lineage and another capable combat machine to boot.

I n mid-1953, using the new Mystère IVB fuselage as a starting point, Dassault's Saint Cloud engineering team developed new wings to create an improved variant which was successively name Mystère XX, Mystère IV B1 and finally Super Mystère B1.

The basic Ouragan layout reached its zenith with the Super Mystère – revised oval nose intake, 45-degree wing sweepback and a full-vision canopy blended into a raised spine.

Thanks to its powerful Rolls-Royce RA.7R Avon engine and those aerodynamic refinements, the first prototype, designated Super Mystère B1 01, became the first aircraft in Western Europe capable of sustained level flight above Mach 1 on March 3, 1955, the day after its first flight, piloted by Paul Boudier.

A series of five SNECMA Atar 101G-powered pre-production aircraft were then built under the designation

DASSAULT SUPER MYSTÈRE B2

Dassault Super Mystère B2, 9, Centre d'Expériences Aériennes Militaires (CEAM), Armée de l'Air, (Military Aeronautical Experimental Centre, French Air Force), Mont-de-Marsan, France, 1958.
CEAM used a varied fleet of aircraft, including several Super Mystères.

▼ DASSAULT SUPER MYSTÈRE B2

Dassault Super Mystère B2, 06, 105 Squadron, Israel Defense Force/Air Force, Hazor air base, Israel, 1960.
Israeli Super Mystères were used operationally in the 1967 and 1973 wars and were also involved in a controversial attack on the USS *Liberty*; this aircraft carries napalm bombs.

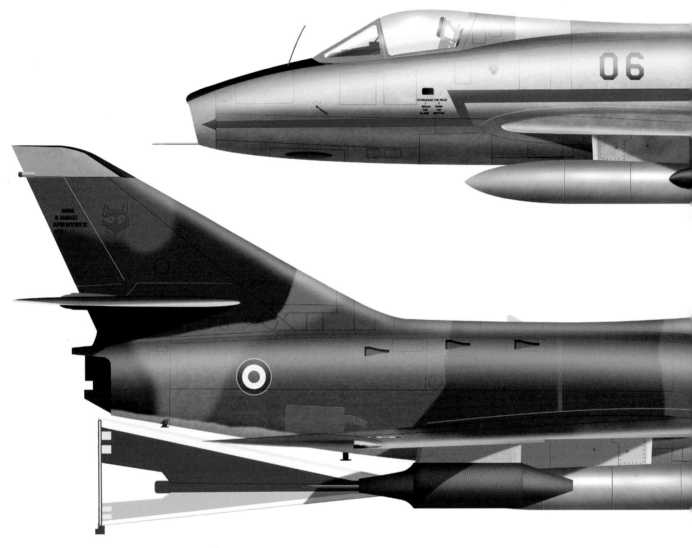

▼ DASSAULT SUPER MYSTÈRE B2

Dassault Super Mystère B2, FAH 2002, Fuerza Aérea Hondureña, (Honduran Air Force), La Ceiba air base, Honduras, 1990.
Honduras acquired its Super Mystères from Israel; the aircraft featured improvements including a non-afterburning version of the Pratt & Whitney J52-P-8A engine and new avionics, being designated in Israel as the IAI Sa'ar. This aircraft is armed with Rafael Shafrir 2 air-to-air missiles and rocket pods.

DASSAULT SUPER MYSTÈRE B2

Dassault Super Mystère B2, 10-SM/21, Escadron de Chasse 1/10 'Valois', SPA 84 'Tête de renard', Armée de l'Air (Fighter Squadron 1/10, Flight 84, French Air Force), 110 air base, Creil, France, 1974.
The Super Mystère served in France until 1974 and during the latter years examples were painted in camouflage colours; this aircraft carries a towed target for air-to-air gunnery practice.

Super Mystère B2 – also known as the SMB2 – and the first of these made its flight debut on May 15, 1956, piloted by Gérard Muselli.

The French government initially ordered 220 SMB2s, then cut that to 178 of which only 154 would eventually be delivered. Early production examples were powered by the afterburning Atar 101G-2, with this later being switched to the improved Atar 101G-3.

The SMB2 was initially armed, as usual, with a pair of DEFA 30mm cannon, plus stores weighing up to 2,680kg on four underwing pylons. The latter could include drop tanks, reconnaissance pods, unguided rocket packs, bombs or even AIM-9 Sidewinder missiles.

Deliveries commenced in 1957 with the last example arriving in 1959. Rapidly switched to the ground-attack role, they would continue in French service until 1974. Two examples had been built with Atar 9B engines in 1958 under the designation Super Mystère B4, but no production order was placed for this variant.

The Israelis bought 18 French-production SMB2s in 1958 and referred to it as the 'Simbad' – based on its 'SMB-Deux' initials. These were formed into two squadrons which became operational in March 1959. They would be engaged in various skirmishes against MiG-17s during the early 1960s and in April 1967 Israel bought another 24 from the French Air Force – just in time for the Six-Day War against a coalition of Arab states, now equipped with the new MiG-21.

On the first day of the conflict, Simbad pilots flew 128 sorties and destroyed dozens of enemy aircraft on the ground, plus five in the air. Having disabled the Arab air forces, they switched to ground-attack the following day – taking on Egyptian armour and artillery. By the end of the war Israel had lost nine Simbads – six of their pilots killed and one captured.

Even after the war, the fighting continued. Another Simbad was lost on December 4, 1968, while attacking Iraqi forces. The pilot survived only to be captured and beaten to death by Jordanian troops.

Meanwhile, France embargoed weapons sales to Israel in the wake of an Israeli commando raid on Beirut airport, leading to the prospect of the surviving Simbads running out of spares. Therefore, the IAF decided to replace the Atar 101G-3s in its aircraft with non-afterburning Pratt & Whitney J52-P-8As taken from its fleet of A-4 Skyhawks. Installing the new engine required airframe modifications which resulted in a longer fuselage. Israeli avionics were also added.

The first Super Mystère fitted with this new powerplant made its flight debut on February 13, 1969. Israel gave the type a new name – Sa'ar, meaning Tempest – and all remaining Simbads, a total of 26,had become Sa'ars by early 1973.

Four years later, in 1977, the IAF sold a dozen Sa'ars to Honduras which would continue to operate them until 1990.

SUD AVIATION
VAUTOUR II

A basic no-frills combat jet, the twin-engine Vautour or 'Vulture' enjoyed a surprisingly long career thanks to its versatility and ability to carry hefty payloads.

1956-1979

▼ SUD AVIATION VAUTOUR IIN

Sud Aviation Vautour IIN, 30-FK/356, Escadron de Chasse Tout-Temp 3/30 'Lorraine', Armée de l'Air, (All-Weather Fighter Squadron 3/30, French Air Force), 112 air base, Reims, France, 1961.
This interceptor version of the Vautour is armed with Matra R511 air-to-air radar-guided missiles.

666

he Société nationale des constructions aéronautiques du Sud-Ouest, aka SNCASO, aka Sud-Ouest, began working on designs for a jet bomber during the late 1940s even as Dassault was developing the Ouragan fighter.

Two half-scale demonstrators were built, the S.O. M1 and S.O. M2, that latter of which was flown with a single Rolls-Royce Derwent engine on April 13, 1949. This led to the construction of the full-scale S.O. 4000 Vautour – a cigar-shaped aircraft with mid-mounted slightly-swept wings powered by two Hispano-Suiza-built Rolls-Royce Nene 102 engines buried within its fuselage.

It first flew on March 16, 1951, but failed to attract a production order.

Sud-Ouest persevered, however, and submitted a revised version to meet a June 1951 French Air Force requirement for a jet platform that could be adapted to fill three roles: ground-attack, level bomber and night fighter.

While it retained the same basic fuselage shape, the new S.O. 4050 Vautour II had a completely revised swept tail fin, 35-degree swept wings, full-vision cockpit canopy and underwing engine pods – freeing up the fuselage interior for additional fuel and an internal bomb bay. The complex undercarriage of the original Vautour was swapped for a straightforward bicycle arrangement with outriggers under the engine pods.

The attack type would be the Vautour IIA, with a single-seat cockpit and four

DEFA 30mm cannon armament. The level bomber was the Vautour IIB with a glazed nose for the addition of a bombardier and the cannon deleted; and the night fighter was the Vautour IIN with a two-seat cockpit, nose radar and four cannon.

All had four underwing stores pylons, the inner pair able to carry 1,250kg each, the outer pair 500kg each. On the Vautour II A and B, these would typically be used to carry a selection of bombs and external fuel

⏶ SUD AVIATION VAUTOUR IIB

Sud Aviation Vautour IIB, 602, Escadron de bombardement 2/92 Aquitaine, Armée de l'Air, (Bomber squadron 2/92, French Air Force), 167 air base, Reggane, Algeria, 1960.
In 1960, Vautours from the EB 2/92 were deployed to Algeria to provide support for the first French nuclear test, Operation Gerboise Bleue, in the Sahara Desert.

tanks. Alternatively, they could carry reconnaissance or electronic countermeasures equipment.

On the Vautour IIN they could carry two Matra R511 air-to-air missiles and (from the early 1960s) two Nord AA-20 AAMs, or two AAMs plus two drop tanks.

The first prototype, a two-seater, made its flight debut on October 16, 1952,

with Jacques Guignard at the controls. Vautour IIA and IIB prototypes were also made, followed by six pre-production machines. These were used to test a variety of alternative engines, including the Rolls-Royce Avon, Armstrong Siddeley Sapphire and the Atar 101, variants of which would eventually be chosen to power all production Vautours.

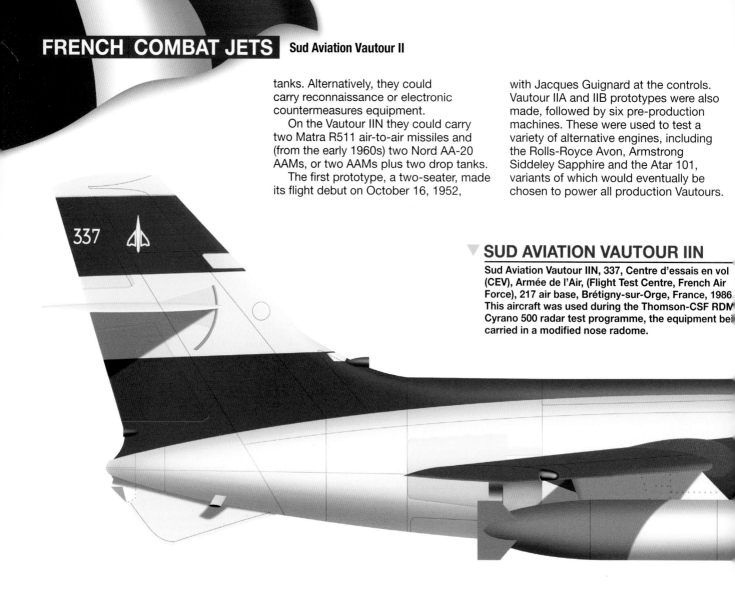

▼ SUD AVIATION VAUTOUR IIN

Sud Aviation Vautour IIN, 337, Centre d'essais en vol (CEV), Armée de l'Air, (Flight Test Centre, French Air Force), 217 air base, Brétigny-sur-Orge, France, 1986. This aircraft was used during the Thomson-CSF RDM Cyrano 500 radar test programme, the equipment being carried in a modified nose radome.

▼ SUD AVIATION VAUTOUR IIA

Sud Aviation Vautour IIA, 09, 110 Squadron, Israel Defense Force/Air Force, Ramat David air base, Israel, 1966. Israel was the only export operator of the Vautour, and employed it in several roles (fighter, attacker, reconnaissance), from 1958 until 1972.

The first production aircraft was a Vautour II A, which made its initial flight on April 20, 1956. However, budget cuts prompted the purchase of 150 Republic F-84F Thunderstreak fighters and 50 RF-84F Thunderflash reconnaissance aircraft rather than a large fleet of Vautours. So only 13 IIAs, 36 IIBs and 63 IINs were made for the French Air Force – a total of 112 aircraft – not including nine prototypes. Sud-Ouest was merged with Sud-Est

to became Sud Aviation on March 1, 1957.

The Vautour II As would never enter French service. The IIBs would however, and from the mid-1960s they could be used to carry a single AN-11 or AN-12 nuclear weapon as the original aerial component of France's nuclear deterrent – the force de frappe. A number would continue in this role up to 1978. Most Vautours, however, were phased out of service much earlier, some being

retained for experimental and trials work.

Israel chose the Vautour to replace its fleet of de Havilland Mosquitos in 1957 and the first example arrived on August 1, 1957. A total of 36 were delivered – 25 IIAs, four IIBs and seven IINs. The type was used extensively throughout the 1960s in a variety of roles, particularly for reconnaissance. The survivors were retired in 1972 and replaced by A-4 Skyhawks and F-4 Phantom IIs.

DASSAULT ÉTENDARD IV

Though built in only small numbers the Étendard IV would serve the Aéronavale, the French Navy's air arm, as a carrier-based strike fighter for nearly 40 years – proving to be both capable and adaptable.

1962-2000

▼ DASSAULT ÉTENDARD IVM

Dassault Étendard IVM, 7, Escadrille 59S, Aéronavale, Marine Nationale (Squadron 59S, Naval Air Arm, French Navy), Hyères naval air base, France, 1991.
A special scheme celebrating 30 years of the Étendard; on the fin are the emblems of all the units that operated the type. Étendard IVMs had a retractable refuelling probe, as shown here.

Dassault developed both single and twin-jet variants of a tactical strike fighter design in 1953 to meet NATO and French Air Force requirements respectively. The basic aerodynamic configuration was initially that of a scaled down Super Mystère but incorporating high lift devices for lower take-off and landing speeds.

The single-engine Mystère XXVI (Étendard VI) for NATO and the twin-engine Mystère XXII (Étendard II) for the French Air Force would ultimately be cancelled. But a third version, the larger and more powerful Mystère XXIV (Étendard IV) fitted with a single Atar 101E, attracted interest from all quarters.

Dassault was awarded a contract to build a prototype in November 1954 and this made its first flight on July 24, 1956, piloted by Georges Brian. It too, however,

would end up being disqualified from the NATO competition and rejected by the French Air Force at the end of 1957.

Meanwhile, the French Navy had asked Dassault to redesign the Étendard IV as a "low-altitude fighter and seaborne attack aircraft" in 1955. The first Étendard IVM prototype, with the M standing for Marine, flew on May 21, 1958, powered by a SNECMA Atar 08B turbojet, and the first pre-production aircraft flew on December 21, 1958.

The production model Étendard IVM had an area-ruled fuselage with side intakes, mid-mounted wings with a 45-degree leading edge sweep, all-moving tailplanes, retractable refuelling probe, licence-made Martin-Baker ejection seat, cockpit pressurisation, Aida 7 navigation radar and SAAB BT9F bombing computer. It also had a catapult hook under the forward corner of each

wing, an arrestor hook and folding wingtips. Armament was two DEFA 30mm cannon under the intakes plus four underwing pylons able to carry various stores including external fuel tanks, Sidewinders or Matra Magics, unguided rockets, bombs or Nord AS.30 air-to-surface missiles. A centreline tank could also be fitted but rarely was.

The sixth production Étendard IVM was used to trial the Étendard IVP reconnaissance configuration with three film cameras in a modified nose plus two more in a removable belly pack. A total of 69 IVMs and 21 IVPs were delivered from 1961 to 1965. With various modifications and modernisations these would serve aboard the carriers *Clemenceau* and *Foch* until 1997 and 2000 respectively. The IVMs saw little or no combat but the IVPs would fly during Middle Eastern conflicts during the 1970s and over Yugoslavia in the 1990s.

▼ DASSAULT ÉTENDARD IVP

Dassault Étendard IVP, 107, Flotille 16F, Aéronavale, Marine Nationale, (Squadron 16F, Naval Air Arm, French Navy), aircraft carrier *Clemenceau* (R98), 1980.
The unit flew the Étendard IVP from 1964 until 2000, when it was disbanded; this aircraft carries a buddy-pack refuelling system.

DASSAULT-BREGUET SUPER ÉTENDARD

The Super Étendard naval strike fighter was arguably France's first truly modern combat aircraft – with multimode radar, a navigation-attack system and the deadly Exocet missile.

1978-2016

▼ **DASSAULT-BREGUET SUPER ÉTENDARD**
Dassault-Breguet Super Étendard Modernisé, 62, Flottille 11F, Aéronavale, Marine Nationale (squadron 11F, Naval Air Arm, French Navy), Ørland air base, Norway, 2007.
The Artic Tiger was the Aéronavale's contribution for the 2007 NATO Tiger Meet.

The Aéronavale began to cast around for something to replace its Étendard IVMs during the late 1960s and initially set its sights on either the Vought A-7 Corsair II or the French-made navalised SEPECAT Jaguar – the Jaguar M.

Dassault, however, argued that an upgraded Étendard IVM, sharing 90% parts commonality with the original aircraft would be a much cheaper option.

The French government agreed and the Super Étendard was selected as the French Navy's new multipurpose strike fighter on January 19, 1973. It was to replace not just the Étendard IV but also the Vought F-8 Crusader fighter and Bréguet 1050 Alizé anti-supmarine warfare aircraft.

A contract for 100 Super Étendards was signed on September 4, 1973, and the 68th Étendard airframe became the Super Étendard 01 prototype, being first flown in modified configuration on October 28, 1974, by Jacques Jesberger. The first production machine was flown on November 24, 1977, again by Jesberger.

It had a SNECMA non-afterburning Atar 8K 50 turbojet, larger engine intakes, a new wing with leading-edge root extensions and increased sweep, and a whole suite of new electronics equipment.

In the nose was a Thomson-CSF Agave I multimode radar optimised for maritime strike, providing both navigation and air combat capabilities. Its inclusion gave the aircraft's nose a distinctive

droop – visually differentiating it from the Étendard IV.

Also included was a SAGEM-Kearfott ETNA navigation-attack system. This brought together a Thomson-CSF head-up display (HUD), radio altimeter, TACAN beacon navigation system, armament control system and navigation display.

Étendard IV features carried over included the two DEFA 30mm cannon, retractable inflight refuelling probe, four underwing pylons able to carry a variety of stores such as bombs, unguided rockets or external tanks, and the rarely used centreline tank attachment point. Apart from the new nose it was difficult to tell the Super Étendard apart from the original Étendard but in reality the

▽ DASSAULT-BREGUET SUPER ÉTENDARD

Dassault-Breguet Super Étendard, 1, Flottille 17F, Aéronavale, Marine Nationale (Squadron 17F, Naval Air Arm, French Navy), *Foch* **aircraft carrier (R99), 1983.**
Super Étendards operated from the aircraft carrier *Foch* **off the coast of Lebanon, supporting the French peacekeeping forces deployed there.**

Dassault- Breguet Super Étendard

▼ DASSAULT-BREGUET SUPER ÉTENDARD

Dassault-Breguet Super Étendard Modernisé, 51, Flottille 17F, Aéronavale, Marine Nationale (squadron 17F, Naval Air Arm, French Navy), Kandahar, Afghanistan, 2008.
Super Étendards were land-based in Afghanistan to conduct operational missions painted in this overall grey colour scheme; this aircraft carries GBU-49 laser guided bombs, Alkan LL5081 chaff and flare dispensers and the Damocles targeting pod.

DASSAULT-BREGUET SUPER ÉTENDARD

Dassault-Breguet Super Étendard Modernisé, 47, Flottille 11F, Aéronavale, Marine Nationale (squadron 11F, Naval Air Arm, French Navy), RAF Fairford, 2005.
A modernised Super Étendard is seen here at the 2005 Royal International Air Tattoo, with new camouflage colours and carrying an Exocet anti-ship missile.

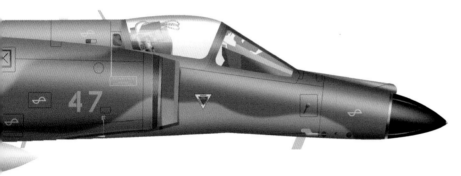

DASSAULT-BREGUET SUPER ÉTENDARD

Dassault-Breguet Super Étendard, 3-A-202, 2da Escuadrilla Aeronaval de Caza y Ataque, Comando de la Aviación Naval Argentina, Armada de la República Argentina (2nd fighter and attack air naval squadron, air naval command, Argentine Navy), Rio Grande naval air base, Argentina, 1982.
Operating from a mainland base, since it was not possible to do so from the aircraft carrier ARA *25 de Mayo*, Argentina's Super Étendards achieved several hits on British ships using the Exocet anti-ship missile; this aircraft is shown with the retractable refuelling probe extended.

aircraft had very little parts commonality – negating the cost benefits originally forecast.

As a result, the original order for 100 examples was cut to just 71. Pilots, however, found the Super Étendard easy to fly and its systems were indeed state-of-the-art for the time. In particular, it was able to carry and launch the Aérospatiale AM39 Exocet anti-ship missile when it entered service in 1979 – targeting it with the Agave radar.

For the anti-ship mission, a Super Étendard would typically carry an Exocet on the inner pylon of one wing with an external fuel tank in the same position on the other wing. The outer pylons would then be used for AAMs or countermeasures and the cannon would be removed to allow space for additional electronics.

The Aéronavale's Super Étendards were upgraded to carry a nuclear payload such as the AN-52 freefall bomb or the ramjet-powered ASMP missile during the early 1980s and the flight configuration used would be similar to that outlined above.

Super Étendards flew airstrikes in support of French peacekeeping forces in Lebanon in September 1983 and five were loaned to Saddam Hussein in 1983 as a stopgap until Exocet-equipped Mirage F1s could be delivered to Iraq in 1985. These were used to attack tankers in the Persian Gulf during the ongoing Iran-Iraq War in 1984 and one was lost in combat.

A programme of modernisation was launched during the late 1980s, resulting in the Standard 2 Super Étendard Modernisé (SEM). This included a new HUD, a flat panel display, hands on throttle and stick (HOTAS) controls and the new Thales Anemone multimode radar with improved jamming resistance and double the range of the old Agave.

The first Standard 2 SEM was flown in October 1990 and the type entered frontline service in June 1993. Standard 3 SEM followed, which included an ATLIS laser targeting pod in the centreline station, and then Standard 4 which offered an updated suite of countermeasures carried in pods attached to new underwing stores pylons fitted inboard of the existing inner pylons.

Standard 4 also enabled the SEM to carry a CRM 280 centreline reconnaissance module. This included an AP 40 panoramic camera and an SDS 250 electro-optic imager and allowed SEMs to take over from the now outdated Étendard IVP fleet.

By the end of 2002, 47 SEMs had been upgraded to Standard 4 and Standard 5 then followed in 2003, bringing night attack capability thanks to the new Damocles targeting pod. Standard 5 SEMs, of which there would be 34, also included night vision goggles, the PCN 90 flight computer and the UNI 140 global positioning system satellite receiver.

▼ DASSAULT-BREGUET SUPER ÉTENDARD

Dassault-Breguet Super Étendard Modernisé, 23, Flottille 11F, Aéronavale, Marine Nationale (squadron 11F, Naval Air Arm, French Navy), *Charles de Gaulle* aircraft carrier (R91), 2010. This Super Étendard received an eye-catching paint scheme to celebrate the centenary of French naval aviation.

▼ DASSAULT-BREGUET SUPER ÉTENDAR

Dassault-Breguet Super Étendard, 4669, Iraqi Air Force, Iraq, 198 During the so-called tanker war of the Iran-Iraq conflict, five Sup Étendards were loaned to Iraq, while the country waited for the delivery of Mirage F1s capable of carrying the Exocet anti-ship missile. Controversy still surrounds the serial numbers of the aircraft concerned.

Aéronavale SEMs were flown into action during the Balkan Wars of the late 1990s and flew missions in Afghanistan from the invasion in 2002 up to 2010. They were then involved in the NATO air offensive over Libya in 2011 as well as missions against the Islamic State in 2015. The type was finally retired in 2016.

The only foreign customer to buy Super Étendards was, famously, Argentina – which ordered 14 examples in 1981. Only five had been delivered, along with five Exocet missiles, when the Falklands War began in 1982 with the French immediately suspending deliveries.

Argentine Super Étendards launched two of the five precious Exocets against HMS *Sheffield* on May 4, 1982, and one hit. Although it failed to explode, it knocked out the vessel's fire-fighting systems, killed 20 crew and led to a blaze which caused severe damage as well as injuring many more crewmen. *Sheffield* eventually sank while under tow as water entered through the hole in her side. A second pair of Exocets were launched against the container ship *Atlantic Conveyor* on May 25, again causing serious damage and killing 12 of the 33 crew. It too eventually sank while under tow.

The fifth and final Argentine Exocet was fired on May 30 but missed. After the war, France delivered the remainder of the Argentine order. Starting in 2009, Argentina paid to have ten of its remaining 11 Super Étendards upgraded to SEM standard but as of 2019 only five had been delivered and even these lacked key parts required to make them airworthy. What's left of Argentina's Super Étendard fleet, modernised and otherwise, was in storage at the time of writing.

DASSAULT-BREGUET SUPER ÉTENDARD

Dassault-Breguet Super Étendard Modernisé, 44, Comando de la Aviación Naval Argentina, Armada de la República Argentina (air naval command, Argentine Navy), 2020.
Argentina acquired five SEMs in 2017; the entry of the aircraft into operational service has reportedly been delayed due to spare parts problems.

DASSAULT
MIRAGE III

Dassault's Mirage III could be regarded as the most successful French combat jet ever made. Fast and extremely capable in a variety of roles, advanced versions and derivatives remain in service today.

1961-NOW

▼ DASSAULT MIRAGE IIIC

Dassault Mirage IIIC, 2-EF/25, Escadron Chasse 1/2 Cigognes, Armée de L'Air (Fighter Squadron 1/2, French Air Force), air base 102, Dijon-Longvic, France, 1967.
Tasked with the high-altitude interception mission, the first Mirage IIICs were armed mainly with a single ventrally-carried Matra R.530 air-to-air missile.

French military aviation was booming in 1953. The Ouragan had been in service for a year, Mystère II prototypes were being tested, Mystère IV prototypes were being tested, a Voutour II prototype was being tested and Dassault was already designing what would become the Super Mystère and Étendard IV.

Against this backdrop, the French government issued a specification for a lightweight all-weather supersonic interceptor. Dassault responded with a delta-wing design powered by two afterburning Turboméca Gabizo engines

and a SEPR rocket motor for extra thrust.

Using its own funds, the company began building a prototype under the designation MD 550 that was powered by a pair of licence-made Armstrong Siddeley MD30R Viper engines. The French government then issued a contract for two rocket-boosted MD 550 prototypes on March 22, 1953 – vindicating Dassault's decision to press ahead without official backing.

As its name suggested, the resulting Mystère-Delta aircraft had a delta wing with 60-degree leading edge sweep and a 5% ratio of wing thickness to chord. It

also had an extremely large tail fin. Roland Glavany took it up for its first flight on June 25, 1955, and during its fourth flight on July 24 managed to reach Mach 0.95 in a dive.

The aircraft then went back to the workshop for six months of fine-tuning, after which it could manage Mach 1.3 in level flight. Further revisions then followed: a swept fin was installed, the engines were fitted with afterburners and new intakes and a SEPR 66 booster rocket was added.

Flown again on May 5, 1956, the aircraft – now renamed Mirage I – could manage Mach 1.6. However, it was clear by now that the type was simply too

DASSAULT MIRAGE III 001

Dassault Mirage III 001, Melun-Villaroche airfield, France, 1956.
This is the first prototype for the Mirage III and it would undergo numerous modifications, particularly in the intake area. Derived from the Mirage I (Mystère Delta), the aircraft was later developed into the Mirage IIIA 01, which featured similar lines to those of the production aircraft.

DASSAULT MIRAGE IIIE

Dassault Mirage IIIE, 4-BJ/619, Escadron Chasse 2/4 La Fayette, Armée de L'Air (Fighter Squadron 2/4, French Air Force), air base 116, Luxeuil, France, 1986.
For the 70th anniversary of the EC 2/4, two aircraft were painted in this special scheme complete with shark mouth.

DASSAULT MIRAGE IIIR

Dassault Mirage IIIR, 560, Direction générale pour l'armement (General Weaponry Directorate), air base 120, Cazaux, France, 2005.
The last flight of a Mirage III in France was made by this aircraft in 2005; it belonged to the DGA, a unit responsible for handling weapons systems for the French armed forces and for export.

DASSAULT MIRAGE IIIEBR

Dassault Mirage IIIEBR (F-103), 4929, 1° Grupo de Defesa Aérea, Força Aérea Brasileira (1st Air Defence Group, Brazilian Air Force), Anápolis Air Base, Brasília, Brazil, 1996.
Brazilian Mirages (locally designated F-103) were upgraded in the early 1990s with new avionics, weapons and canards; this aircraft is armed with Rafael Python 3 air-to-air missiles.

small. It's payload was limited to just a single air-to-air missile. The second prototype commissioned was to have been powered by the originally specified Turboméca Gabizo engines under the designation Mirage II, but instead the programme was cancelled.

Meanwhile, at the end of 1955 Dassault had begun work on a larger delta-wing fighter that was to be powered the new afterburning SNECMA Atar 08. It would also incorporate the 'area ruling' concept developed in America during the early 1950s and implemented on the Convair F-102 – resulting in a 'wasp waist' fuselage.

The first prototype of the new fighter, Mirage III 001, made its flight debut on November 17, 1956, piloted by Roland Glavany, and managed to reach Mach 1.52 on its seventh flight.

A SEPR rocket motor was installed and in April 1957 the French government ordered ten pre-production Mirage IIIAs. The prototype made a public appearance at the 22nd Paris Air Show on June 11 and during its 78th flight, on September 19, 1957, it managed to reach Mach 1.8 in level flight using the rocket booster. Two weeks later upped this to Mach 1.89 but the Dassault team realised that the aircraft's jet inlets were holding it back.

As a result, its inlets were modified to incorporate movable half-cone centrebodies. The French referred to these as 'souris' or 'mice'.

With the design now a clear success, the French government placed an order for 100 full production examples of the Mirage IIIC interceptor as well as, on February 25, 1958, 63 two-seat Mirage IIIB trainer variants, including the first prototype. The IIIB fuselage was lengthened to accommodate the second crewman and its radio equipment was moved to the nosecone, replacing the radar system.

FRENCH COMBAT JETS | Dassault Mirage III

Of the 63 IIIBs ordered, five would be IIIB-1 trials aircraft, ten would be IIIB-2(RV) inflight refuelling trainers with dummy nose probes and 20 would be Mirage IIIBEs. The latter type – which would become a hit on the export market under a variety of designations – effectively comprised the Mirage IIIB

two-seater airframe but fitted with the multirole combat capabilities of the later Mirage IIIE.

The first Mirage IIIA pre-production machine was test flown for the first time on May 12, 1958, with Glavany again at the controls. It was 2m longer than the Mirage III 001, its wing had 17.3% more

▼ DASSAULT MIRAGE IIICZ

Dassault Mirage IIICZ, 804, 2nd Squadron, South Africa Air Force, Hoedspruit Air Base, South Africa, 1980.
South African Mirages were involved in the Border War; this aircraft carries the dual fuel rocket pod Matra JL100.

surface area with thickness to chord reduced to 4.5% and it was powered by the latest afterburning Atar 09B. The SEPR rocket motor installation was included and it had a Thomson-CSF Cyrano Ibis air intercept radar, avionics and a drag chute to shorten its landing distance.

Before long, Glavany was able to take the first Mirage IIIA briefly up to Mach 2.2 in level flight – making it the first European-produced aircraft to go beyond Mach 2.

The Mirage IIIC single-seat interceptor was just under half a metre longer than the IIIA and it had the same engine with a variable exhaust. Armament was the usual two 30mm DEFA cannon beneath the engine intakes plus three stores

pylons – one under each wing and a third beneath the fuselage. Two more underwing pylons were soon added for a total of five stores positions.

While the outer pylons were generally reserved for AAMs – first Sidewinders and later Magic missiles – the other three could carry various combinations of bombs, unguided rocket packs and drop tanks. Later stores included laser target designators, Martel air-to-surface missiles, cluster bombs and Durandal anti-runway penetration munitions.

The Mirage IIIC retained the ability to carry a SEPR rocket booster but seldom did. The space was more often used to carry extra fuel and the rocket nozzle was initially replaced by a ventral fin, this in

turn later being swapped for an airfield arrestor hook.

The prototype Mirage IIIB first flew on October 20, 1959, piloted by René Bigand, and the last Mirage IIIA was delivered in December 1959. On April 6, 1960, the French government ordered both multirole/strike and reconnaissance variants as the Mirage IIIE and Mirage IIIR respectively.

The IIIE was slightly longer than the IIIC thanks to an additional 30cm forward fuselage extension which allowed more room for fuel and more space for the avionics bay behind the cockpit.

It also had an improved Atar 09C engine with petal type variable exhaust, Thomson-CSF Cyrano II dual mode air/

DASSAULT MIRAGE IIIBZ

Dassault Mirage IIIBZ, 818/R, 2nd Squadron, South Africa Air Force, Ysterplaat Air Base, Cape Town, South Africa, 1967.
The SAAF's 2nd Squadron was equipped with Mirage IIIs in 1963 and operated them until 1990; in the early years, the aircraft were flown in natural metal finish.

DASSAULT MIRAGE IIIEE (C.11)

Dassault Mirage IIIEE (C.11), 111-01, Ala 11, Ejército del Aire (Wing 11, Spanish Air Force), Manises Air Base, Valencia, Spain, 1986. Spanish Mirage IIIs were operated from 1970 until 1991, being replaced by F/A-18 Hornets. This aircraft carries the AIM-9J Sidewinder air-to-air missile.

ground radar, a radar warning receiver system (RWR) with tailfin antennas, and in many cases – though not all – a Marconi continuous wave Doppler navigation radar radome on the fuselage underside below the cockpit. Armament was two DEFA cannon and five stores pylons were available with a total carrying capacity of four tonnes.

And the Mirage IIIE airframe provided the basis for the Mirage IIIR, the usual radar nose being swapped for one fitted with up to five OMERA film cameras.

The first production standard Mirage IIIC made its flight debut on October 9, 1960, flown by Jean Coureau. He took the first Mirage IIIE prototype up for its debut flight on April 1, 1961 and was

also at the controls of the first Mirage IIIR during its maiden flight on October 31, 1961. Deliveries of Mirage IIICs to the French Air Force had commenced on July 7, 1961, and the type entered full operational service on December 19 of that year. A total of 95 were delivered and the Mirage IIIC would continue in French service until 1988. The total number of IIIBs delivered to the French Air Force, including the prototype, came to 63.

The first Mirage IIIE full production model was delivered to the French Air Force in January 1964. A total of 192 IIIEs would eventually be bought by France, plus 52 Mirage IIIRs, including a pair of prototypes. The Mirage IIID was the two-seat trainer version of the IIIE but the type was only ordered by export customers. In some instances, when customers bought a 'IIID' they were actually buying a IIIBE.

ISRAEL

The Israeli Air Force followed the Mirage's development with keen interest and placed an initial order for 24 Mirage IIICs in 1959, with the export version for Israel being redesignated Mirage IIICJ. The order was increased to 72 in 1961, with the first aircraft being delivered to Hazor AFB on April 7, 1962. Two reconnaissance Mirage IIICJ(R)s were received in March 1964 and three two-seater Mirage IIIBJs were received 1966, another following in 1968. Israel would later fabricate its own camera noses, modifying four or more IIICJs to carry them – supplementing the IIICJ(R)s. In IAF service, the Mirage III was known as the 'Shahak' or 'Sky'.

IAF Mirages engaged enemy aircraft in combat at least four times between August 1963 and March 1965 but struggled to make a 'kill'. It was eventually realised that the IIIC had been designed to intercept Soviet bombers, so the shells of its DEFA cannon were optimised to explode inside a large target. When they hit a small target, they simply passed straight through and out the other side, exploding a short distance away and causing minimal damage. The Israelis addressed this problem by loading rounds with zero delay fuses which exploded on impact.

The Mirage III was also the first IAF fighter capable of carrying air-to-air missiles – the French Matra 530 and Israeli Shafir I, but these proved so unreliable that pilots preferred to continue using guns.

Now carrying new ammo, four IAF Mirages went into action against four Syrian MiG-21s on July 14, 1966, and Captain Yoram Agmon of 101st squadron managed to down one with his cannon. It was the first kill for a Mirage and the first time an Israeli fighter had shot down a MiG-21. Just over a month later on August 15 another Mirage downed another MiG-21 over the Sea of Galilee.

▼ DASSAULT MIRAGE IIIEA

Dassault Mirage IIIEA, I-018, Grupo 8 de Caza, Fuerza Aérea Argentina (Fighter Group 8, Argentine Air Force), Río Gallegos air base, Argentina, 1982.
During the Falklands War in 1982, these Mirages were deployed from their usual air base near Buenos Aires to forward positions. Despite being closer to the theatre of operations, the aircraft still had only a few minutes over the islands for combat operations; this aircraft carries Matra Magic 1 AAMs.

▼ DASSAULT MIRAGE IIIEA

Dassault Mirage IIIEA, I-011, Grupo 8 de Caza, Fuerza Aérea Argentina (Fighter Group 8, Argentine Air Force), Tandil air base, Argentina, 2015.
Several Argentine Mirages received special paint schemes for their final flight; this was one of them, featuring tail-art which references the type's years of operations within the FAA. It also has an emblem celebrating 100 years of military aviation in Argentina.

DASSAULT-GAF MIRAGE IIIO

Dassault-GAF Mirage IIIO, A3-54, 75 Squadron, Royal Australian Air Force, Butterworth Air Base, Malaysia, 1981.
A number of alternative colour schemes for the RAAF Mirage fleet were evaluated; this one was among those not adopted.

DASSAULT MIRAGE IIID

Dassault Mirage IIID, A3-112, Aircraft Research and Development Unit (ARDU), Royal Australian Air Force, Laverton, Victoria, Australia, 1985.
ARDU used a fleet of several aircraft including the famous Fanta-can Mirages. This aircraft carries the Matra TK500 fuel/bomb pod.

DASSAULT MIRAGE IIICJ

Dassault Mirage IIICJ Shahak, 259, 101 Squadron, Israel Defence Force – Air Force, Hatzor Air Base, Israel, 1968.
Israeli Mirages were used with great success during the Six-Day War; this aircraft's kill marks testify to that. The aircraft is armed with the indigenous Rafael Shafrir 1 and French Matra R.530 air-to-air missiles.

A Jordanian Hawker Hunter was shot down by Mirage in mid-November 1966, followed by two Egyptian MiG-19s on November 29 – one of them destroyed using a Matra 530 for Israel's first ever air-to-air missile victory.

However, it was the events of April 7, 1967 – the first day of the Six-Day War – that would cement the Mirage III's reputation. Syrian and Israeli ground forces had exchanged fire during the morning and IAF Ouragans, Mystères, Super Mystères and Mirages commenced ground strikes at 1.32pm in the afternoon.

The attack was broken off when approaching Syrian MiGs were detected and Mirages from 101st Sqn were vectored in to engage them. At 1.58pm captains Iftah Spector and Benyamin Romah took on two MiG-21s over the Syrian town of Kuneitra and a dogfight ensued. Spector managed to down his opponent quickly but Romah's fled. Giving chase, Romah got a short burst of cannon fire into him as he reached Damascus and this was enough to make the kill. Then, at 3.52pm, Major Ran Peker of the 119th Squadron destroyed another MiG-21 with a cannon hit to its fuel tank.

By 4.16pm only six Mirages were left in the air – two each from the 101st, 117th and 119th squadrons. They were making their way back to base when, at 4.27pm, they encountered four MiGs over the Golan Heights. Major Ezra Dotan and Captain Avraham Lanir of 117th Sqn got two of them and Captain Avner Slapak of 101st Sqn got another. A total of six kills in one day. By the end of the war, Mirages had shot down 48 enemy aircraft.

And the kills would keep coming over subsequent years. Eventually, however, the Mirage IIICJ was replaced by F-4 Phantoms and F-15 Eagles, with the type finally being retired from the IAF in 1982.

SOUTH AFRICA

There would be only three Mirage IIIC export customers – Israel, South Africa and Switzerland – but these few opened the door to many further exports for the IIID and IIIE as well as licence production abroad. South Africa bought 15 Mirage IIICs under the designation IIICZ along with three IIIBZ two-seaters. These entered service in 1963. Further orders were then placed for at least 16 IIIEZs, three IIIDZs, four IIIRZs and 12 IIID2Zs.

During the 1980s the South African government, unable to purchase new military aircraft thanks to a UN arms embargo, worked with the Atlas Aircraft Corporation to upgrade its existing fleet of Mirage IIIs into a new advanced type along the lines of the IAI's Nesher and Kfir upgrades. This produced three variants – the two-seat Cheetah D, the interim single-seat Cheetah E and the later single-seat Atlas Cheetah C.

These aircraft were refurbished to zero flight hours condition, around 50% of the original airframe being replaced with new parts. Non-moving canards were fitted slightly aft of the engine inlets, new

▼ ATLAS CHEETAH E

Atlas Cheetah E, 831, 5th Squadron, South Africa Air Force, Louis Trichardt air base, South Africa, 1991. The Atlas Cheetah was the result of a South African modernisation programme of its Mirage III fleet; the first variant created was the Cheetah E, developed as an interim fighter until the definitive C variant was ready for use. This aircraft carries the indigenous Denel V3B air-to-air missile.

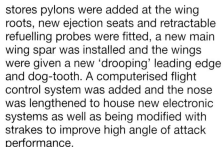

DASSAULT MIRAGE IIIEL

Dassault Mirage IIIEL, 504L, Lebanese Air Force, Rene Mouawad Air Base, Kleyate, Lebanon, 1969. Lebanon operated its Mirages for about ten years from 1968 on. They were then put into storage and later sold to Pakistan.

DASSAULT-F+W MIRAGE IIIS

**Dassault-F+W Mirage IIIS, J-2325, Fliegerstaffel 16, Schweizer Luftwaffe/Forces Aériennes Suisses/ Forze Aeree Svizzere (Air Squadron 16, Swiss Air Force), Sion Airport, Switzerland, 1998.
Swiss Mirages were produced under licence. Later on the aircraft's service, a modernisation programme saw the addition of canards and upgraded avionics; this aircraft carries AIM-9 Sidewinders and has a series of rocket bottles installed on the lower rear fuselage for extreme short take-offs.**

stores pylons were added at the wing roots, new ejection seats and retractable refuelling probes were fitted, a new main wing spar was installed and the wings were given a new 'drooping' leading edge and dog-tooth. A computerised flight control system was added and the nose was lengthened to house new electronic systems as well as being modified with strakes to improve high angle of attack performance.

The Cheetah D and E retained the original Atar 9C turbojet but the Cheetah C received the more powerful Atar 9 K50. A total of 16 Cheetah Ds, 16 Cheetah Es and 36 Cheetah Cs were reportedly completed – more than the total number of Mirage III airframes known to have been originally purchased by South Africa.

The Cheetah Es were retired in the 1990s as the C started to become available. Five were bought by Chile in 2003 as a source of spares for its Mirage 5-based ENAER Panteras prior to their retirement in 2006. Most Ds and Cs were retired in 2008 when South Africa purchased the SAAB Gripen, a pair of Ds continuing to serve as systems testbeds for the state-owned Denel Aviation organisation.

Ecuador then bought 10 ex-SAAF Cheetah Cs and two Cheetah Ds in 2010, retiring them in 2021. American firm Draken International announced in December 2017 that it would buy 12 ex-SAAF Cheetahs to use in the adversarial role for training military pilots.

SWITZERLAND
A single Mirage IIIC was bought by Switzerland in 1961 after a deal was signed allowing the Swiss to build 100 Mirage IIIs under licence for the Swiss Air Force. These aircraft, designated Mirage IIIS, were made by F+W Emmen, now part of government-owned RUAG.

It had been proposed that the 100 aircraft would each be able to perform the attack, intercept and reconnaissance roles using different loadouts without the need for different airframes but this proved too difficult and costly to accomplish – particularly given the other customisations required by the Swiss government. These included airframe and undercarriage strengthening, the addition of crane lifting points, retractable nosecones and longer nosewheel legs.

They would also be fitted with new cockpit interiors and equipment including the American Hughes TARAN-18 radar, allowing them to carry AIM-4 Falcon missiles, RWRs and the option to carry a reconnaissance pod and/or a SEPR rocket motor. Eventually F+W built just 36 Mirage IIIS interceptors, these entering service in 1967. Switzerland also bought a single Mirage IIIR reconnaissance aircraft from France, then manufactured 17 of their own as the Mirage IIIRS. These entered service in 1969.

An upgrade programme in 1988 saw canards designed by RUAG fitted to the Swiss Mirage IIIs as well as a Martin-

Baker ejection seat and a TRACOR AN/ALE-40 chaff/flare dispenser. The last examples were retired in 2003.

AUSTRALIA

An initial order for 30 Mirage IIIO types for the Royal Australian Air Force was placed on December 15, 1960, with the stipulation that the first two would be supplied complete from France, six would be supplied as knockdown kits and two more would be supplied simply as parts.

The remainder would be manufactured locally in Australia.

Further orders followed and once the process began Dassault supplied a dozen aircraft as knockdown kits, then 25 complete fuselages. The rest of the aircraft were Australian-made in three variants – the Mirage IIIO(F), Mirage IIIO(A) and Mirage IIID. The IIIO(F) was optimised as a fighter, the IIIO(A) for attack and the IIID was the two-seat trainer variant. The IIIO(A) was similar

▼ DASSAULT-GAF MIRAGE IIIO

Dassault-GAF Mirage IIIO ROSE I, 90-586, No.7 Squadron, Pakistan Air Force, Masroor Air Base, Pakistan, 2013.

This Mirage was acquired from Australia and upgraded to ROSE 1 (Retrofit Of Strike Element) standard; this upgrade featured improvements to avionics, a new radar and a fixed refuelling probe, among other modifications. It carries the AIM-9 Sidewinder.

to the III(F) but carried the Cyrano IIB Doppler radar and altimeters.

Production was carried out by the Australian Government Aircraft Factory (GAF) and Commonwealth Aircraft Corporation, with the latter making major subassemblies including the Atar engines and flight surfaces and the former making the rest as well as carrying out final assembly.

The first Aussie-made Mirage took its debut flight in March 1963 and eventually Australia would operate a total of 116 Mirages – 49 IIIO(F)s, 51 IIIO(A)s and 16 IIIDs. A handful of IIIO(A)s were converted to carry a single nose-mounted camera in place of the Cyrano radar for reconnaissance.

Between 1967 and 1979, all surviving IIIO(F)s were converted to IIIO(A) standard and redesignated Mirage IIIO(FA). The type was retired in 1988 with Pakistan buying 55 examples, 43 single-seaters, seven two-seaters and five further airframes to be cannibalised for spares, in 1990.

PAKISTAN
Over the course of several decades, Pakistan has accumulated numerous Mirage airframes. An initial order was placed in 1967 for 18 Mirage IIIEPs, three Mirage IIIDPs and three Mirage IIIRPs. A further ten IIIRP2s were delivered between 1977 and 1978.

As mentioned, Pakistan then acquired 50 airworthy Australian Mirage IIIOs in

1990. Eight of these were put into service immediately while another 33 were upgraded to incorporate a HUD, HOTAS controls, multi-function display, radar altimeter, SAGEM nav/attack system, inertial navigation and GPS, RWR, and a suite of electronic countermeasures – as well as flares and a chaff dispenser. On top of all this, the FIAR Grifo M3 radar was added in 1999.

Pakistan then bought ten Mirage III types from Lebanon in 2000 plus 15 IIIEEs and five IIIDEs from Spain 2003 to use for spares. There would be still more changes in 2011, with the Pakistani Mirages upgraded to carry the Hatf-VIII Ra'ad cruise missile and South African-made refuelling probes. Since then

▲ ATLAS CHEETAH C
Atlas Cheetah C, 358, 2nd Squadron, South Africa Air Force, Makhado air base, Limpopo, South Africa, 2007. The Atlas Cheetah was operated by the 2nd Squadron until it was replaced by the SAAB Grippen; it carries the medium range radar-guided Denel R-Dart air-to-air missile.

modifications have been made which allow the Pakistani Mirages to carry newer weapons such as China's PL-12 AAM.

LEBANON

A dozen Mirage IIIs – ten IIIEL single seaters and two IIIBL trainers – were delivered to Lebanon in 1968. Not long afterwards, in 1969, the Lebanese aircraft were reportedly the subject of a plot to steal a Mirage III. Agents from the Soviet embassy in Beirut approached a former Lebanese Air Force pilot and asked him to get in touch with his old comrades to obtain details about the Mirage's radar and avionics. The pilot did so, but his contact within the Lebanese Air Force

▶ ATLAS CHEETAH D

Atlas Cheetah D, 861, 2nd Squadron, South Africa Air Force, Makhado air base, Limpopo, South Africa, 2004.
The famous 'bandit' aircraft as seen at the Africa Aerospace Defence 2004 Exhibition.

▶ ATLAS CHEETAH C

Atlas Cheetah C, FAE-1362, Escuadrón de Combate N.° 2112, Ala 21, Fuerza Aérea Ecuatoriana (Combat squadron 2112, Wing 21, Ecuadorian Air Force), Taura air base, Ecuador, 2020.
Ecuador received the Atlas Cheetah in 2011; the aircraft were retired in 2021.

told his superiors what had happened. They advised the contact to get in touch with the Soviets directly, who then suggested that the contact should defect via Turkey to Baku in Soviet Azerbaijan during a long-range training flight in a Mirage III. He was to be paid $3m US dollars for delivering the aircraft and the Soviets pledged to keep his family safe in Switzerland.

During the final meeting between the contact and the Soviets in an apartment building, the Lebanese police broke in and a firefight erupted. Two Lebanese personnel were injured, as were Vladimir Vassoleev, an engineer at the commercial mission of the Soviet embassy, and Aleksander Komiakov, a colonel of the Soviet Committee for State Security. The Lebanese police were victorious, however, capturing both Vassoleev and Komiakov as well as the corrupt former Lebanese Air Force pilot. After protests from Moscow, Vassoleev and Komiakov,

still on stretchers, were loaded onto an Aeroflot plane and sent back to Russia.

Lebanon's Mirage IIIs remained in service for a decade but were then grounded and put into long-term storage due to a lack of funds to keep them flying. The stored aircraft were eventually sold to Pakistan in 2000.

SPAIN
Spain bought 31 Mirage IIIs in 1968 – 24 IIIEEs (locally designated C.11) and seven

▼ **DASSAULT MIRAGE IIIEP**
Dassault Mirage IIIEP, 67-115, No. 5 Squadron 'Falcons', Pakistan Air Force, Rafiqui Air Base, Pakistan, 1971. Pakistani Mirages were involved in the 1971 war, performing both air-to-air and air-to-ground missions.

DASSAULT MIRAGE IIIC

Dassault Mirage IIIC, 10-RO/55, Escadron de Chasse 2/10 'Seine', Armée de L'Air (Fighter Squadron 2/10, French Air Force), air base 110, Creil, France, 1979.
This pink Mirage was the result of a prank by the personnel of EC 1/10; there would be payback a year later.

DASSAULT MIRAGE IIIO

Dassault Mirage IIIO, A3-44, 77 Squadron, Royal Australian Air Force, Williamtown Air Base, Australia, 1984.
This Mirage IIIO, in the original camouflage colours, is seen carrying Matra 530 and AIM-9 missiles; the type would be replaced by the F/A-18 Hornet in RAAF service.

DASSAULT MIRAGE IIING

Dassault Mirage IIING (Nouvelle Generation), Le Bourget Air Show, Paris, France, 1983.
The Mirage IIING was a programme initiated by Dassault to incorporate several upgrades into the venerable Mirage III. It included new canards and fly-by-wire systems alongside numerous other improvements to aerodynamics, avionics and engine. It was flown as a single prototype in May 1981 but it did not attract any customers.

IIIDEs (CE.11) – with the first example delivered in June 1970. A plan was drawn up in 1990 to upgrade 23 Spanish Mirage IIIs to C.15 standard but instead they were retired the following year.

ARGENTINA

Negotiations between Dassault and Argentina for the purchase of 12 Mirage IIIs – ten Mirage IIIEA single-seat interceptors and a pair of Mirage IIIDA two-seat trainers began in 1968, with the purchase being finalised in 1970. Deliveries then commenced in 1972 and a second contract was signed in 1977 for another seven single seaters, bringing the overall total to 19. This was raised to 21 when another pair of trainers were bought in 1980, with deliveries in 1982. Two IIIEAs being lost during the Falklands War in 1982 – one shot down by a Royal Navy Sea Harrier and the other lost to friendly fire. The remaining Argentine Mirage IIIs were eventually retired in 2015.

BRAZIL

The Brazilian government signed up to buy 16 Mirage IIIs on May 12, 1970. The order would comprise a dozen single-seat Mirage IIIEBRs and four two-seat Mirage IIIDBRs – to be designated F-103E and F-103D respectively in Brazilian service. The first aircraft arrived in October 1972 and the last in May 1973. Attrition took its toll over the years and a steady stream of ex-French Air Force Mirage IIIs went to Brazil during the 80s and 90s. Four F-103Es (Dassault gave these replacements the designation Mirage IIIEBR-2) arrived in 1980, two F-103Ds in 1984, two more F-103Es in 1988, two more in 1989 plus two F-103Ds, another pair of F-103Es in 1998 and lastly two more F-103Ds in 1999. This brought the combined total number of Mirage IIIs received by Brazil up to 32.

A limited upgrade programme was carried out starting in 1989, with all F-103s getting canards and minor structural and mechanical modifications. The Brazilian fleet was eventually retired on December 31, 2005.

VENEZUELA

Seven Mirage IIIs were ordered by Venezuela as part of a package which also included nine Mirage 5s. All seven were Mirage IIIEV interceptors and were delivered in May 1973. See the Mirage 5 chapter for more details.

DASSAULT
MIRAGE 5

33

1968-NOW

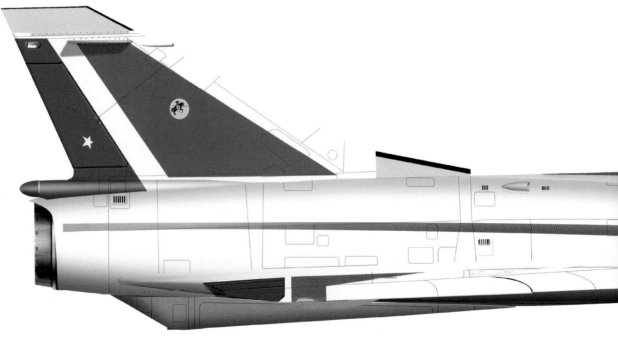

Dassault stripped the Mirage III of its radar to create a simplified and inexpensive modern fighter – which proved to be exactly what a number of air forces around the world were looking for.

With the Mirage III already proving to be a success, Israel approached Dassault to create a simplified attack variant. Dassault took the job and the new version, based on the IIIE, was given the designation Mirage 5.

Its features were set out by the company's engineers on July 9, 1965 – the complex, expensive and maintenance-intensive radar was replaced with basic electronic nav/attack equipment in a nosecone made around 50cm longer, creating extra internal space, and more attachment points were added for underwing loads.

These two simple changes effectively increased fuel capacity by 32% and allowed the Mirage 5 to carry a wide variety of payload options unavailable to the IIIE. Israel signed an order for 50 examples on April 7, 1966.

The initial Mirage 5 prototype was first flown on May 19, 1967, by Hervé Leprince-Ringuet. In addition to the longer nose and two extra stores pylons – fitted at the rear junctions of the fuselage and wings and taking the total number of pylons up to seven – its pitot tube was relocated from the tip of the nose to just below it. Internal armament continued to be the ubiquitous pair of 30mm DEFA cannon.

However, French President Charles de Gaulle placed the Israeli Mirage 5s under embargo on June 3, 1967, due to rising tensions in the Middle East. Dassault continued to build the aircraft anyway however, and placed completed airframes in storage. Eventually Israel was given a refund on them and they were passed to the French Air Force under the designation Mirage 5F. These would be the only Mirage 5s to enter French service.

It has been suggested that France simultaneously and covertly supplied 50 more knocked down Mirage 5 kits to Israel in crates, which would eventually be built as IAI Neshers (see below). Israel, however, claims to have manufactured these aircraft itself from scratch after obtaining a full set of original blueprints – although exactly how those blueprints were obtained remains unclear.

▲ DASSAULT MIRAGE 5F

Mirage 5F, 13-SG/33, Escadron de Chasse 3/13 Auvergne, Escadrille 4 GC II/9 – Morietur, Armée de l'Air (Fighter Squadron 3/13, Flight 4 GC II/9, French Air Force), air base 132, Colmar-Meyenheim, France, 1989.
The French Air Force received the Mirage 5s originally destined for Israel; this aircraft carries the Matra TK500 fuel/bomb pod and the Phimat chaff dispenser.

▼ DASSAULT MIRAGE 5F

Dassault Mirage 5F, 13-PE/41, Escadron de Chasse 2/13 Alpes, Armée de l'Air (Fighter Squadron 2/13, French Air Force), air base 132, Colmar-Meyenheim, France, 1987.
The patrouille Métro Mike demonstration team was formed within EC 2/13 and performed from 1987 until 1994.

▶ DASSAULT-SABCA MIRAGE 5BR

Dassault-SABCA Mirage 5BR, BR-22, 42nd Squadron, Force Aérienne Belge/ Belgische Luchtmacht/ Belgische Luftmacht (Belgian Air Force), Florennes air base, Belgium, 1984.
Belgian Mirages were built locally under licence by the Sociétés Anonyme Belge de Constructions Aéronautiques (SABCA); this 42nd Squadron example wears a special paint scheme commemorating the 30th anniversary of the unit.

▼ DASSAULT MIRAGE 5EAD

Dassault Mirage 5EAD, 501, II Shaheen Squadron, Abu Dhabi Air Force, Al Dhafra Air Base, Abu Dhabi, United Arab Emirates, 1978.
Mirages were originally operated by the Abu Dhabi Air Force into the 1990s, before transitioning into a new service: the United Arab Emirates Air Force.

DASSAULT MIRAGE 50 PANTERA

Dassault Mirage 50 Pantera, 503, Grupo 4, Fuerza
Aérea de Chile, (group 4, Chilean Air Force), Carlos
Ibañez air base, Punta Arenas, Chile, 2007.
The upgraded Mirage 50 Pantera had improvements
to its aerodynamics, structure, avionics and weapons.
This aircraft carries Rafael Python 3 AAMs and laser-
guided IAI Griffin bombs.

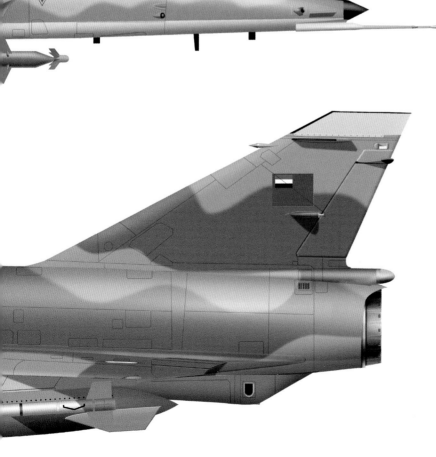

The Mirage 5 would go on to enjoy
great success on the export market,
both in its original form and as renamed
'copies': the IAI Nesher, IAI Kfir and Atlas
Cheetah. It should also be noted that the
Mirage 5 really differed very little from the
Mirage III and with some derivatives the
line between what constitutes a Mirage III
and a Mirage 5 becomes rather indistinct.
It could be argued that all Mirage 5s,
Mirage 50s, Neshers, Kfirs and Cheetahs
are really Mirage III subvariants.

There were also numerous one-offs
and prototype offshoots from the Mirage
5 family – too many to detail here. These
included the French-Swiss 'Milan'
development with pop-out 'moustache'
foreplanes from 1968 to 1972 and the
Mirage IIING (see previous chapter) of 1982
with updated aerodynamics and avionics.

ISRAEL

Officially, Israel Aircraft Industries (IAI)
started work on manufacturing an
unlicensed copy of the Mirage 5, based
on technical documents supposedly
obtained prior to de Gaulle's arms
embargo, in 1969. Unofficially, it has been
claimed that the blueprints were either
obtained by Israeli spies or else were
passed to Israel covertly – perhaps even
by de Gaulle himself.

Whatever the case, the aircraft that
IAI would build was essentially a Mirage
5 but featuring Israeli-made avionics, a
British Martin-Baker zero-zero ejection
seat, and weapons systems which
enabled it to carry a wider range of
ordnance than the original French design
allowed.

The prototype, named Nesher or
'Vulture', made its first flight on March
21, 1971, and deliveries to the IAF
commenced in May 1971. A total of 51
single-seat Nesher As were made plus
ten two-seater Nesher Bs.

During the Yom Kippur War of 1973,
Neshers were responsible for shooting
down dozens of Syrian, Egyptian and
Libyan aircraft. On a number of occasions
the Israeli Mirage clones came face to
face with Libyan Mirage 5s and at least
two of the latter were shot down by
Neshers during the course of the war.

But Israel certainly wasn't finished with
the Mirage 5. Following the success of
the Nesher, it was decided that a more
capable variant should be produced
in order to maintain Israel's qualitative
superiority over its opponents.

Strenuous efforts were made to glean
information about the latest Mirage
5 variants and assistance from other
international operators of the type and
experiments began to determine where
improvements could be made.

Re-engining the basic Mirage 5
airframe with a General Electric J79 made
good sense since it was more powerful
than the Atar and Israel had begun to
acquire J79-powered F-4 Phantom IIs
from the US in 1969 as well as a licence
to build the engine locally.

▼ IAI KFIR C2

IAI Kfir C2, FAE905, Escuadrón 2113,
Fuerza Aérea Ecuatoriana (Squadron 2113,
Ecuadorian Air Force), Taura air base,
Ecuador, 1996.
Ecuadorian Kfirs saw combat during the
Cenepa Border conflict with Peru; an A-37
kill was awarded to one of its pilots.

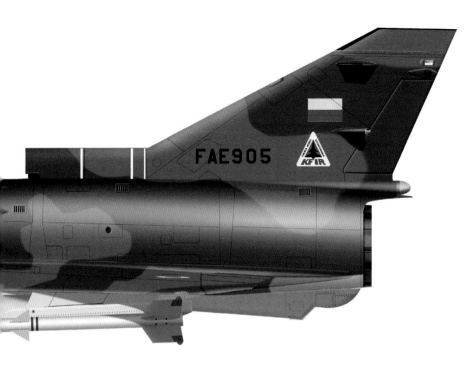

DASSAULT MIRAGE 5COAM

Dassault Mirage 5COAM, 3030, Escuadrón Combate 212, Grupo de Combate 11, Comando Aéreo de Combate No. 1, Fuerza Aérea Colombiana (Squadron 212, Combat Group 11, 1st Air Combat Command, Colombian Air Force), Captain Germán Olano Moreno air base, Cundinamarca, Colombia, 2008.
This upgraded Mirage 5COAM carries IAI Griffin laser-guided bombs; Colombian Mirages saw action against insurgent groups.

IAI KFIR C1

IAI Kfir C1, 750, 101 Squadron, Israel Defense Force/ Air Force, Hatzor air force, Israel, 1979.
Based on the Mirage 5, the Kfir featured modifications such as a new engine (General Electric J79 turbojet), avionics, aerodynamics and weapons; the first variant did not feature the canards and nose fences seen on later models. Israeli Kfirs first entered service with 101 Squadron.

This necessitated a slightly shortened and widened fuselage plus bigger air intakes and a new inlet at the base of the tailfin for the afterburner.

The new type was named Kfir and the IAI Kfir C1 entered service with the IAF in 1975. This was swiftly followed by the Kfir C2 which featured a host of aerodynamic improvements – most notably a pair of large fixed canards on the sides of the air intakes, fences on the nose and 'dogtooth' wing leading edges.

A trainer variant, the Kfir TC2, was given a longer lower nose to provide the pilot with better visibility and a reconnaissance type, the RC2, was fitted with a camera nose.

The Kfir's first combat mission was flown on November 9, 1977 – an airstrike against a training camp in Lebanon – and its first kill was made on June 27, 1979, when a Kfir C2 shot down a Syrian MiG-21. All IAF Kfir C2s were upgraded to C7 standard during the early 1980s. This extensive series of modifications included new J79-GE-J1E engines, improved avionics and two additional hardpoints under the intakes. Two-seaters receiving the updates were given the designation Kfir TC7.

Israel's own Kfirs were retired in the late 1990s.

PERU
The government of President Fernando Belaúnde Terry signed a deal to buy 16 Mirage 5P aircraft in 1967 and nine further contracts would then follow up to 1977, eventually bringing the total number purchased up to 37: 22 5Ps, 10 5P3s (fitted with new navigation systems and radio altimeters), four two-seater 5DPs and one two-seater 5DP3. Training of Peruvian pilots began in France during December 1967 and the first Mirage 5P was flown for the first time in Peru by a Peruvian pilot on July 18, 1968. The Mirage 5Ps would be flown in combat during a conflict with Ecuador in 1981 and in 1982 Peru sold ten of its Mirage 5Ps to Argentina. The remaining Mirage 5Ps would participate in combat against Ecuadorian forces again in 1995 and some would be upgraded to 5P4 standard with HUDs, HOTAS controls, laser rangefinders, inflight refuelling probes and new avionics before eventually being retired in October 2001.

BELGIUM
The Belgian government decided to buy 106 Mirage 5s from Dassault in 1968 but wanted to have them licence-built locally by SABCA. The SABCA factory at Haren would make the components and the plant at Gosselies airfield near Charleroi would carry out final assembly. The Atar engines, meanwhile, would be made by FN Moteurs at the Liège plant. Avionics would be supplied separately by American companies.

Dassault supplied a single Mirage 5BA ground-attack aircraft, a single Mirage 5BD two-seat trainer and three Mirage 5BR reconnaissance aircraft as examples. SABCA then made 62 5BAs, 15 5BDs and 23 5BRs itself.

Twenty low-hours 5BAs and five 5BDs were subjected to the Mirage Safety Improvement Programme at the end of the 1980s, which saw them fitted with modernised cockpits, new ejection seats, laser rangefinders and fixed canards. Once this had been completed, all 20

aircraft were sold on to Chile together with four standard 5BRs and a single standard 5BD.

PAKISTAN
Having already been a Mirage III operator, it wasn't much of a leap for Pakistan to then buy Mirage 5s when they became available. The initial purchase was 28

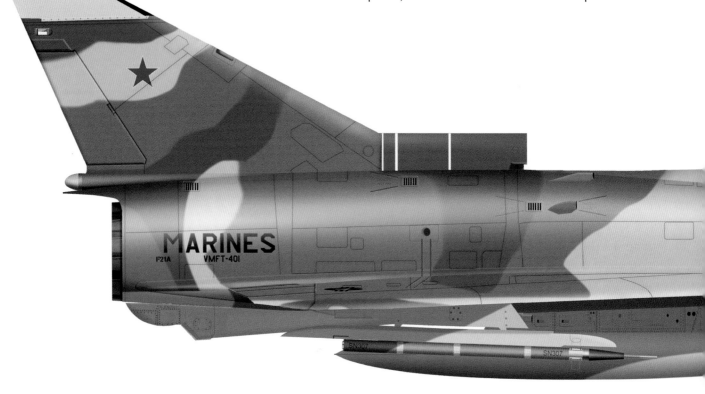

▶ IAI KFIR C7

IAI Kfir C7, SFM721, No. 10 Squadron, Sri Lanka Air Force, Katunayake air base, Sri Lanka, 2019.
Sri Lankan Kfirs were used against Tamil separatists; this aircraft carries the IAI Griffin laser-guided bomb. In 2021, an agreement was reached with Israel to upgrade the aircraft to Block 60 standard.

Mirage 5PAs and these were followed by 18 Mirage 5PA2s. This variant differed in having Agave radar installed. Then 12 examples of a specialised Exocet-launching anti-shipping variant, the Mirage 5PA3, were purchased.

By the early 1980s, Pakistan had bought around 90 Mirages of all types. Starting in 1990, the Pakistani military began buying up second-hand Mirages from Australia, Lebanon, Libya and Spain (see Mirage III chapter) and

upgrading them along with its own fleet under Project ROSE (Retrofit Of Strike Element) at the Pakistan Aeronautical Complex, working with French firm SAGEM.

First phase ROSE aircraft had a HUD fitted along with HOTAS controls, a modern cockpit layout, modernised navigation with GPS, defensive countermeasures systems and a FIAR Grifo M multimode radar.

ROSE II included the installation of a

Forward-Looking Infrared (FLIR) imager and a laser rangefinder – accommodated within a fairing under the cockpit. These aircraft also got a low-level flight system and a new targeting system. ROSE III provided a similar loadout but with improved avionics.

A number of Pakistani Mirages were also upgraded to include inflight refuelling probes. At the time of writing, Pakistan had acquired more than 250 Mirage airframes and many of these remained in service. However, plans had been

◀ IAI KFIR C1P

IAI Kfir C1P (F-21A Lion), 03, VMFT-401, US Marine Corps, MCAS Yuma, Arizona, USA, 1988.
A small number of Kfirs were operated by the US Navy and USMC for adversary training in the late 1980s, receiving the designation F-21. The aircraft were based on the earlier C1P variant and had a different canard among other changes.

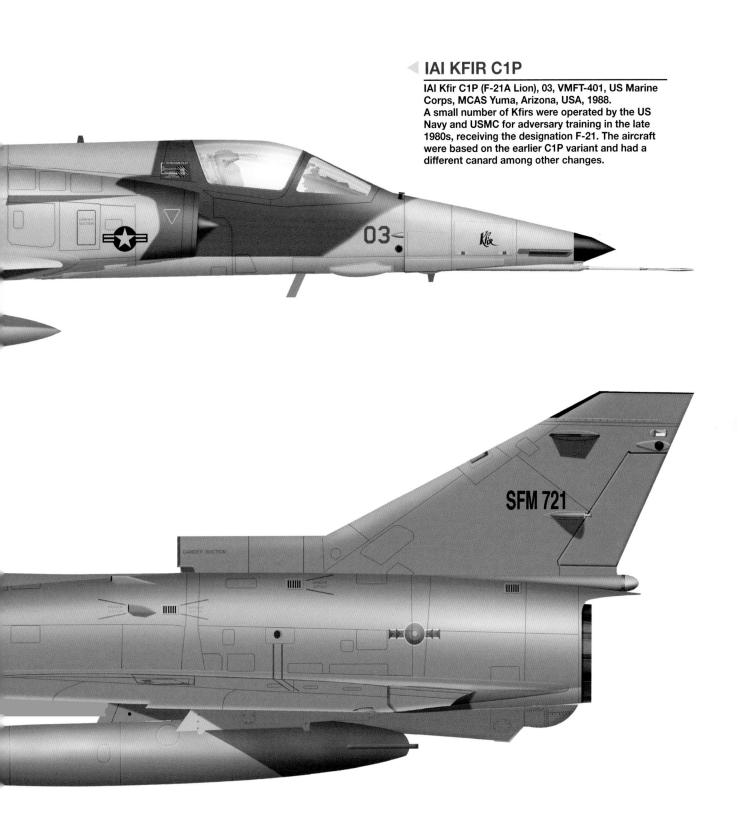

unveiled to retire the Mirages and replace them with Chinese JF-17s.

LIBYA

Colonel Muammar Gaddafi overthrew Libya's King Idris in a coup d'état on September 1, 1969, and quickly moved to distance his regime from both the UK and the US while simultaneously fostering closer relations with France.

Consequently, an order for 110 Mirage 5s was placed by Libya in January 1970. Gaddafi would later loan two squadrons of these aircraft to Egypt for use during the Yom Kippur War of October 6 to October 25, 1973. One squadron was flown by Libyan pilots, the other by Egyptians. These aircraft were returned to Libya after the war.

Libya's remaining Mirages were retired in 2008 and sold to Pakistan as spares.

COLOMBIA

The F-86 Sabres and F-80 Shooting Stars received by the Fuerza Aérea Colombiana (FAC – Colombian Air Force) during the 1950s under the US Military Assistance Program had all been

▷ DASSAULT MIRAGE 5SDE

Dassault Mirage 5SDE, 9126, 236th Fighter Ground Attack Brigade, Egyptian Air Force, Birma/Tanta air base, 1989.
The EAF had a large fleet of Mirage 5s, using them in conflicts with Israel and participating in the Iran-Iraq war; this aircraft carries Matra Magic 2 missiles.

▷ DASSAULT MIRAGE 5G2

Dassault Mirage 5G2, 503, Escadron Chasse 1-02, L'armée de l'Air Gabonaise (Fighter Squadron 1-02, Gabonese Air Force), air base 02, Mvengue-Franceville, Gabon, 1985.
Mirage 5s were the mainstay of the AdlAG combat force until the arrival of Mirage F1s.

retired by 1968 and the United States was refusing to sell military aircraft to Colombia. As such, Colombia looked to Europe for a way to rearm and Dassault won an order for 14 Mirage 5COA single-seat fighters, two 5COD two-seater trainers and two 5COR reconnaissance aircraft in 1970. Deliveries began on January 1, 1972, and concluded on July 17, 1973.

FAC Mirages saw action against guerrilla forces within Colombia throughout the remainder of the 1970s and in 1981 the Colombian government began negotiations to purchase a dozen IAI Kfir C2s from Israel as well as getting its remaining Mirage 5s upgraded. However,

the US vetoed the sale of the necessary engines to Colombia and the deal ground to a halt. However, America finally relented in October 1987 and Congress approved the deal in April 1988. Colombia signed up to buy 12 IAI Kfir C2s and a single Kfir TC7 but allowed an option for 12 additional aircraft to expire.

The deal also involved upgrading both the single-seat Kfirs and a dozen surviving Mirage 5 airframes up to C7 standard, the latter to be redesignated 5COAM and 5CODM for single- and two-seaters respectively. An additional plan to retrofit the Mirage 5s with GE F404s or J79s to match the Kfirs was cancelled due to cost.

The upgrade work commenced during 1988 and was completed in 1990. The first Kfirs arrived on April 28, 1989, and both Kfirs and Mirages were sent into combat on December 10, 1990, to bomb the town of Casa Verde, headquarters of the guerrilla group FARC, in support of ground forces as part of Operation Colombia.

A further round of upgrades commenced in February 2001, including night vision systems and electronics upgrades allowing the Mirages and Kfirs to deploy smart weapons as well as Chilean-made Cardoen

bombs. The two-seaters were fitted with a cockpit laser designator system to direct IAI Griffin laser-guided bombs.

This was the prelude to another large-scale military campaign against FARC in central Colombia's demilitarised zone. A series of FARC targets were hit around the city of San Vicente del Caguán on February 21, 2002, with the Mirages and Kfirs striking bridges, runways, camps, drug-production labs and infrastructure. Attacks continued sporadically up to

2007, with most missions being flown at night.

A contract for 10 new Kfir C7s, three TC7s and one non-flying Kfir C7 for spares was signed in 2008, with these aircraft replacing the Mirage 5s that were still in service. Again, the contract included upgrades for the new aircraft and bringing all remaining Kfirs from the original batch up to C10 standard – which included the Elta EL/M-2032 radar. Seven of the new Kfirs were upgraded to C10

▷ IAI NESHER

IAI Nesher, 525, 144 Squadron, Israel Defense Force/
Air Force, Hatzor air base, Israel, 1973.
IAI Neshers were basically Mirage 5s, although their
exact origin is still a matter of much controversy;
the aircraft would enjoy a successful career, being
the mount of several kill-scoring Israeli pilots. This
aircraft is armed with Rafael Shafrir 2 AAMs.

▽ DASSAULT MIRAGE 5DR

Dassault Mirage 5DR, 306, Libyan Arab Republic
Air Force, Gamal Abdel Nasser air base, Tobruk,
Libya, 1982.
Libya was a major operator of the Mirage 5,
acquiring several variants. These saw action
against Egypt in border clashes after the 1979
peace accords between that country and Israel.

standard and the remaining three were taken up to C12, which was effectively a C10 without the radar. The two-seaters were also upgraded to C12.

The first new Kfir arrived in April 2009 and following the familiar pattern, strikes against FARC began on September 22, 2010. The Mirage 5COAM and CODM were retired in December 2010 but further anti-FARC operations were conducted in 2011 and 2012 using the Kfirs. By 2015 all C12s had been upgraded to C10 standard, leaving Colombia with 18 Kfir COAs, as they continue to be known today.

VENEZUELA
The Venezuelan government ordered 16 Mirages for the Fuerza Aerea Venezolana in 1971: six Mirage 5V single-seaters, which arrived in November 1972, a trio of two-seat 5DVs delivered in February 1973 and the previously mentioned seven Mirage IIIEVs which arrived in May 1973.

Attrition was reportedly very high and by 1989 only eight of the original 16 machines remained. A programme of refurbishment was then devised, with the aircraft set to receive canards, new Atar 9K-50 engines, a HUD,

Cyrano IVM3 radar, RWR, AN/ALE 40 chaff/flare dispensers and inflight refuelling probes. This package was to bring the aircraft up to what was dubbed Mirage 50EV/50DV standard (see the Chile entry below for more on the Mirage 50).

One aircraft was lost in an accident on October 19, 1990, so only seven received the upgrades. Venezuela then also purchased six new 50EVs and one new 50DV two-seater.

Venezuela decided to start buying Russian aircraft in the early

2000s and the Mirages were retired in December 2009, with three single-seat 50EVs and three two-seater 50DVs being donated to Ecuador.

EGYPT
Alongside Pakistan, Egypt has operated Mirages for decades and continues to do so. When President Nasser died in 1970, his successor Anwar Sadat switched

allegiances from the Soviet Union to the United States and Soviet advisors were expelled in 1972. This paved the way for Egypt to begin buying Western military equipment.

However, the first Mirage order for the Egyptian Air Force was actually placed by Saudi Arabia. The Saudis ordered 32 Mirage 5SDE single-seaters and six Mirage 5SDD two-seat trainers

▼ DASSAULT MIRAGE 5P4

Dassault Mirage 5P4, 110, Escuadrón Caza 611, Fuerza Aérea del Perú (Fighter Squadron 611, Peruvian Air Force), Chiclayo air base, Peru, 1986.
One of several upgrades made to the Peruvian Mirages, the 5P4 had a fixed inflight refuelling probe as well as avionics and weapons improvements. This aircraft carries the Soviet-made AA-2 Atoll air-to-air missile.

▼ DASSAULT MIRAGE 50EV

Dassault Mirage 50EV, 2353, Grupo Aéreo de Caza 11, Aviación Militar Bolivariana (Fighter Air Group 11, Venezuelan Air Force), El Libertador air base, Palo Negro, Venezuela, 2009.
Venezuelan Mirages were modified to Mirage 50 standard with upgraded avionics, a new engine and canards; this aircraft carries the Exocet anti-ship missile.

on Egypt's behalf in 1972. Deliveries commenced in 1973 and were completed in 1975.

Saudi Arabia then bought Egypt another 14 Mirage 5SDEs in 1975, with deliveries taking place in 1977, and that same year bought eight more 5SDEs plus six reconnaissance 5SDRs in 1980. Meanwhile, Egypt itself bought 54 more Mirage 5SDEs, six more 5SDDs and six more 5SDRs between 1974 and 1980.

Contrary to the original stripped-back cost-cutting ethos of the Mirage 5 concept, all Egyptian 5SDEs came with Cyrano IV radar. As a result, Egypt was able to use them for both air defence missions, using cannon and Matra missiles, and ground-attack with bombs and rockets. Egypt's Mirages were flown in the ground-attack role in support of Egyptian army units during a short border war with Libya during 1977.

The signing of the Camp David accords between Sadat and Israeli Prime Minister Menachem Begin on September 17, 1978, put an end to Saudi Arabia's financial support and a last batch of 16 Mirage 5E2s that had been ordered on Egypt's behalf were paid for by Egypt itself. The 5E2 came with an enhanced navigation/attack system including SAGEM ULISS 81 inertial navigation as well as Aida RO radar, a HUD, and a Thomson-CSF TMV630 laser rangefinder and marked target seeker.

Egyptian Air Force Mirage 5SDEs carrying ALQ-234 ECM pods on their centreline pylons were sent to Iraq for six weeks in March 1986 to support the Iraqi

Air Force as it fended off Iranian attacks. While the 5SDE's ECM systems were somewhat effective against Iranian F-4s, they didn't work so well against Iran's F-14A Tomcats and Iran reported two Mirage 5SDEs shot down on March 14 – one by a Tomcat and one by an F-4E.

Egypt bought three Mirage IIIEs and three IIIBE conversion trainers from the French Air Force to replace their losses. And in the 1990s they received Zaire's surviving Mirage 5M/5DM airframes to break for spares.

A deal was reportedly signed between the Egyptian and Pakistani

governments in November 2000 for Pakistan Aeronautical Complex to overhaul and upgrade 45 5SDEs, 13 5E2s six 5SDRs and five 5SDDs. Three years later, SAGEM was hired to modernise 24 Mirage 5s for Egypt under what was labelled the Horus Programme. This work, which involved a complete avionics overhaul, was carried out between 2006 and 2008. Meanwhile, Egypt had purchased Abu Dhabi's 19 surviving Mirage 5s to break for spares.

The remaining Egyptian fleet had itself been retired by 2019 and Egypt was

▷ DASSAULT MIRAGE 5DM

Dassault Mirage 5DM, M201, Armée de l'Air Zaïroise (Zaire Air Force), Kamina air base, Zaire, 1977.
Zaire operated a squadron of Mirage 5s from the late 1970s until the late 1980s.

▷ DASSAULT MIRAGE 5PA3

Dassault Mirage 5PA3, 19-449, No. 8 Squadron Haiders, Pakistan Air Force, Masroor air base, Pakistan, 2017.
The Mirage 5PA3 variant has a maritime strike role and is equipped with Agave radar and the Exocet anti-ship missile.

reportedly attempting to sell 36 of them to Pakistan.

ZAIRE
The African nation of Zaire, now the Democratic Republic of Congo, agreed to buy 14 Mirage 5M single seaters and three Mirage 5DM two-seaters in May 1974. Two of the latter were delivered to Kinshasa in October 1975. The first 5Ms arrived in March 1976 and eventually Zaire would receive 11 5Ms and all three 5DMs for a total of 14 Mirage 5s, having run out of funds to buy the remaining three 5Ms. During 1977 and 1978 the Zairian pilots flew their Mirage 5s in the Shaba wars against rebel fighters invading from

Angola but they proved ill-suited to the extremely hot and dusty conditions, suffering jammed guns and bombs that failed to explode.

Only seven 5Ms and one 5DM remained by 1988, whereupon Dassault bought them back and then, as mentioned, resold them to Egypt for spares.

ABU DHABI
A dozen Mirage 5AD single-seat fighter-bombers and three 5DAD two-seat trainers were bought by Abu Dhabi in 1972. A further 14 single-seat radar-carrying Mirage 5EAD aircraft were purchased later along with three Mirage 5RAD reconnaissance variants for a total

of 32. Plans were laid to have Pakistan overhaul 26 airframes in December 1987 but the UAE was unable to obtain sufficient spare parts and only four aircraft were refurbished.

Eleven more were eventually overhauled in France. Overall, 13 aircraft were lost in service and the remaining 19 airframes were sold to Egypt in 2004.

GABON
Being a former French colony, Gabon naturally looked to France when it came to purchasing modern aircraft for its small air force during the early 1970s. As a result, a contract

for three Mirage 5G single-seaters and two 5DG two-seaters was signed in 1975.

Deliveries began in 1978 and Gabon later received four additional Mirage 5G2 aircraft fitted with laser rangefinders – two new builds and two ex-5M aircraft originally constructed for Zaire but never delivered. Gabon also received a pair of new Mirage 5DG2 two-seaters, one in 1984 and 1985, bringing the total number of Mirages operated by the Gabonese up to 11.

Some eight airframes were still in service during the 2010s but all have since been retired.

ARGENTINA

Lacking the funds to buy more Mirages from France, Argentina instead purchased 24 single-seat Neshers plus a pair of two-seaters from IAI in 1978 and called them 'Daggers'. A second contract was signed in 1980 for 11 more single-

▼ IAI DAGGER

IAI Dagger, C-418, Grupo 6 de Caza, VI Brigada, Fuerza Aérea Argentina, (6 Fighter Group, VI brigade, Argentinian Air Force), Puerto San Julián airport, Santa Cruz, Argentina, 1983.
Argentinian Daggers (IAI Neshers) were employed during the Falklands War in 1982; this aircraft has mission markings applied after the conflict.

seaters and another pair of two-seaters, with deliveries taking place in 1981. This gave Argentina a total of 39 Daggers. The single-seaters flew a total 153 sorties against British forces during the Falklands War and managed to damage at least six vessels including HMS *Antrim*, *Ardent*, *Arrow*, *Brilliant*, *Broadsword* and *Plymouth*. In return, 11 Daggers were lost in combat – nine of them shot down by Royal Navy Sea Harriers.

After the war, Argentina bought ten Mirage 5Ps from Peru and operated them under the name 'Mara'. The surviving Daggers were upgraded to Kfir C2 standard and became known as 'Fingers'. All Argentine Mirage derivatives had reportedly been retired by the end of November 2015.

CHILE
Seventeen Mirage 50s were bought for the Chilean Air Force in 1980 as tensions between Chile and Argentina rose over the islands in the Beagle Channel. The Mirage 50, a late development of the Mirage 5, included the more powerful Snecma Atar 9K-50 engine and a new Cyrano IV radar system. Six of Chile's airframes were Mirage 50C attack aircraft, eight were Mirage 50FC interceptors and three were Mirage 50DC two-seat trainers with downrated Atar 9C-3 engines.

Sometime later, 15 of these aircraft including two of the trainers were upgraded by local company ENAER, in cooperation with the Israelis, to create the ENAER Mirage 50CN Pantera or 'Panther'. The Pantera had a new Kfir style nose, upgraded avionics, canards and other aerodynamic alterations. During the 1980s, Chile bought 20 upgraded

▶ IAI KFIR COA (C10)
IAI Kfir COA (C10), FAC3048, Escuadrón de Combate 111, Comando Aéreo de Combate No. 1, Fuerza Aérea Colombiana (Combat Squadron 111, Air Combat Command 1, Colombian Air Force), Captain Germán Olano Moreno air base, Cundinamarca, Colombia, 2017.
This upgraded Kfir carries Rafael Python 4 and Derby air-to-air missiles.

Mirage 5BA/5BD aircraft from Belgium, as mentioned previously, and operated them as the Mirage M-5M Elkan.

All Chilean Mirage 5 derivatives had been retired by the end of 2007.

ECUADOR
The Ecuadorian Air Force's first experience of a Mirage 5-based type came in 1981 when Ecuador ordered ten refurbished ex-IAF Kfir C2s and two TC2s from Israel.

These were then delivered from 1982 to 1983. During the Cenepa War between Ecuador and Peru in 1995, an Ecuadorian Kfir C2 shot down a Peruvian Cessna A-37B Dragonfly using a Shafrir 2 missile.

Ecuador then bought three more C2s and another TC2 in 1996. In 1999, it bought two C10s and a number of its C2s were upgraded to C10 standard.

In 2008, Ecuador's fleet was supplemented by six Mirage 50EV/50DV

▽ IAI DAGGER

DASSAULT-SABCA MIRAGE 5
Dassault-SABCA Mirage 5, BA-60, MIRSIP, Le Bourget Air Show, Paris, France, 1993.
SABCA created the Mirage System Improvement Program (MirSIP) to upgrade Belgium's Mirage 5s; the improved structural, avionics and weapons would be implemented, not on the Belgian aircraft but on the Chilean Elkans.

aircraft from Venezuela. These served until their retirement in 2014 but, as mentioned earlier, Ecuador still retains its Kfirs and a small Mirage III-based Atlas Cheetah fleet.

UNITED STATES
The US Navy and Marine Corps leased 25 Kfir C1s under the F-21A designation in 1985 for use as adversaries in dissimilar air combat training. Unlike earlier C1s, there were fitted with narrow canards and rectangular strakes to improve manoeuvrability at low speeds. All the aircraft were returned in 1989. However, US civilian defence contractor Airborne Tactical Advantage Company (ATAC) continues to operate a number of F-21 Kfirs today.

SRI LANKA
Six Kfir C2s and a single TC2 were bought by Sri Lanka in 1995 and nine more Kfirs, including some C7s, had been purchased by 2005. Two C7s were destroyed on the ground when LTTE rebels attacked the Sri Lanka Air Force (SLAF) base at Katunayake, which is part of Bandaranaike International Airport, on July 24, 2001. Three more were lost in accidents during the Sri Lankan Civil War and another pair were destroyed in a mid-air collision during an air show in March 2011. An deal with IAI to renovate five SLAF Kfirs was announced in June 2021. Today the Sri Lanka Air Force operates six C2s, two C7s and two TC2s.

▼ IAI DAGGER

IAI KFIR RC.2
IAI Kfir RC.2, 451, 143 Squadron The Smashing Parrot, Israel Defense Force/Air Force, Uvda air base, Israel, 1987.
143 Squadron was the last operational IDF/ AF unit to fly the Kfir; this aircraft featured an interchangeable nose section containing reconnaissance cameras.

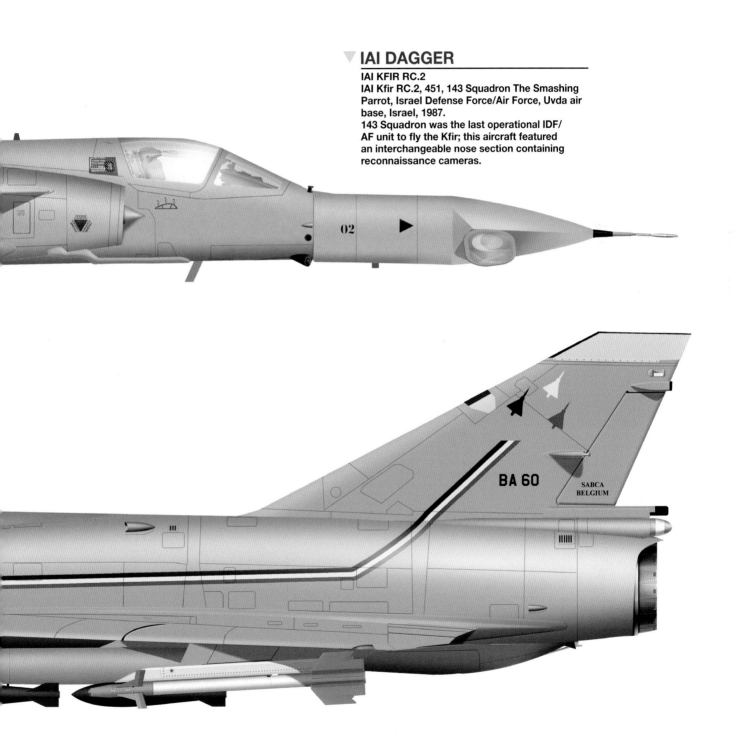

DASSAULT
MIRAGE IV

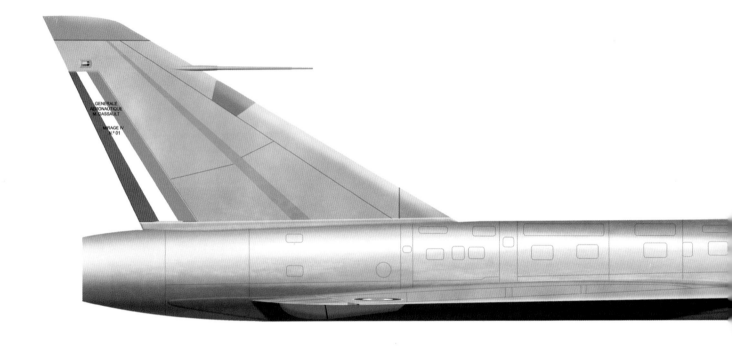

GENERALE
AERONAUTIQUE
M. DASSAULT

MIRAGE IV
N° 01

1964-2005

GENERALE
AERONAUTIQUE
M. DASSAULT

MIRAGE IVA
N.° 36

Impressively sleek and elegant, the Mirage IV bomber/reconnaissance aircraft was built in only small numbers and primarily for a cold war mission it thankfully never had to fulfil.

The events of the Suez Crisis caused France to re-evaluate its approach to nuclear weaponry. The French felt that they needed their own nuclear weapons, independent of America and NATO, and when they had them the ponderous subsonic Vautour IIB would clearly be inadequate as a delivery system.

A requirement for a replacement was issued in 1956 and Sud Aviation put forward proposals for an enlarged 'Super Vautour'. Dassault meanwhile began work on its own submission, submitted to the French government in early 1957. This was to be a scaled up Mirage III, able to manage a sustained cruise at

Mach 2. A Mirage IV powered by two Pratt & Whitney J75 turbojets was initially proposed but a smaller Atar-powered design was eventually chosen for development on March 20, 1957.

The Atar 09C-powered Mirage IV 01 prototype was first flown on June 17, 1959, by Roland Glavany and for its third flight René Bigand displayed it at the Paris Air Show. The specification for the first production type, the Mirage IVA, was set down in October 1959 and on September 15, 1960, the Mirage IV 01 set a new world record for a 1,000km closed circuit flight with an average speed of 1,820km/h (1,130.9mph).

Three pre-production machines

followed, with the first flying on October 12, 1961. An order for 50 Mirage IVA bombers was placed on May 29, 1962, followed by an order for 12 more on November 4, 1962. The first full production Mirage IVA flew on December 7, 1963, and the type officially entered service with the French Air Force in 1964. Production would continue into November 1966 with just the 62 aircraft originally ordered plus the prototype and pre-production machines being made.

The Mirage IVA's layout was similar to that of the Mirage III but scaled up 50%. It had two engines instead of one and two crew seated in tandem on licence-made Martin-Baker zero-zero

▽ DASSAULT MIRAGE IV

Dassault Mirage IV 01, Centre d'Essais en Vol, Armée de l'Air (Flight Test Centre, French Air Force),125 air base, Istres, France,1960.
The prototype for the Mirage IV had several external differences to the production aircraft, the most visible being the lengthened fin.

▽ DASSAULT MIRAGE IV

Dassault Mirage IV, 36, Escadron de bombardement 1/91 'Gascogne', Armée de l'Air (Bomber squadron 1/91, French Air Force), 185 air base, Hao, Tahiti, French Polynesia,1966.
During Operation Tamoure, two Mirage IVs, supported by a Boeing C-135F tanker, deployed from metropolitan France to the Centre d'expérimentation du Pacifique (French Polynesia) to test an experimental AN-21 atomic bomb; the bomb is carried semi-recessed in the fuselage.

ejection seats in a climate-controlled cabin. Landing gear was a two-wheel nosewheel and four wheels on each main gear bogey. The low-mounted wing had the same 60-degree sweep as the Mirage III but had a thinner thickness-to-chord ratio of 3.8% at the root.

Fuel was held in the wings and tailfin as well as the centre fuselage, leaving no room for an internal bomb bay. There was a refuelling probe on the fuselage nose tip. Fully laden take-off required disposable RATO boosters, four under each wing to the rear, and there was a brake parachute in a tail fairing for landing.

Avionics included a Thomson-CSF DRAA 8A navigation radar, Marconi Doppler navigation system, Dassault flight

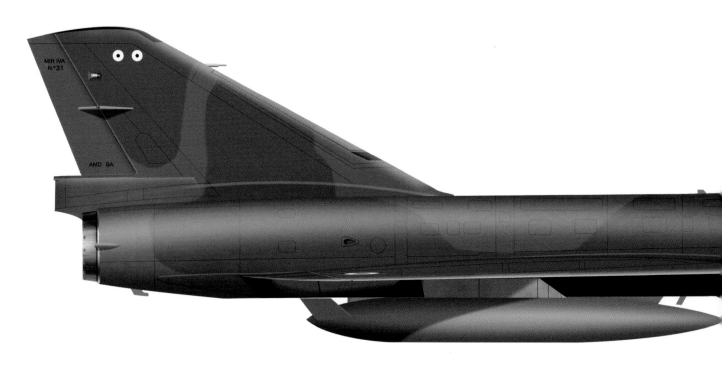

▼ DASSAULT MIRAGE IVP

Dassault Mirage IVP, CF/59, Escadron de Reconnaissance Stratégique 1/91 'Gascogne', Armée de l'Air (strategic reconnaissance squadron 1/91, French Air Force), 118 air base, Mont-de-Marsan, France, 2005.
C'est fini: the last operational Mirage IVs were retired in 2005; this aircraft received a special paint scheme for the occasion.

computer, SFENA autopilot, RWR, IFF and VHF/UHF radios. Under the nose was an OMERA Robot strike camera and there were two pylons under each wing, the inner ones usually for drop tanks and the outer ones for countermeasures. The nuclear weapon, an AN-22 bomb, fitted into a fuselage recess. Alternatively, the IVA could carry six 1,200kg conventional bombs or a quartet of AS-37 Martel anti-radar missiles.

The IVA was the first European military jet capable of sustaining Mach 2 flight for more than 30 minutes.

In 1972, the French government had a dozen IVAs upgraded to IVR standard – the only difference being the wiring necessary to carry a reconnaissance pod in place of the AN-22. The pod, known as CT-52, could be fitted with a variety of cameras and imagers.

Eighteen IVAs were upgraded to IVP status starting in 1982, with the ability to carry the ASMP ramjet-powered standoff missile instead of the AN-22. Other changes included new Thomson-CSF ARCANA pulse-Doppler radar with

ground-mapping, dual SAGEM ULISS inertial nav units, new RWR and new ejection seats.

All but five Mirage IVs were retired in July 1996, replaced in the nuclear delivery platform role by the Mirage 2000N. The five remaining IVPs continued in the strategic reconnaissance role until June 2005, three of them performing high-altitude high-speed overflights of Yugoslav territory during the NATO air campaign against Yugoslavia in 1999.

▼ DASSAULT MIRAGE IVA

Dassault Mirage IVA, BD/31, Escadron de Reconnaissance et d'Instruction, Armée de l'Air (reconnaissance and training squadron, French Air Force), 125 air base, Istres, France, 1986. Mirage IVAs were used in Operation Tobus to gather information following the French attack on the Ouadi Doum airstrip against Libyan forces.

DASSAULT
MIRAGE F1

Developed to succeed the Mirage III, the Mirage F1 was both more manoeuvrable and more capable. Flown into combat time and again, it would prove to be one of the Cold War era's most potent fighting machines.

1973-NOW

In early 1963, the French Air Force general staff prepared a specification for a low-altitude all-weather interceptor able to use improvised air strips – which necessitated a particularly low landing speed.

Dassault responded with a design dubbed Mirage IIIF: a development of the Mirage IIIE with a SNECMA/Pratt & Whitney TF106 engine, a new shoulder-mounted high-lift non-delta wing and low-set tailplanes. The two-seater version was dubbed the Mirage IIIF2 and three prototypes were ordered for the French Air Force in 1965.

Meanwhile, using company funds, Dassault simultaneously designed the Mirage IIIE2 – a lightweight single seater fitted with the wing and tailplane arrangement from the IIIF2. This design was intended as a simple Mach 2 fighter for export.

At around the same time, the company was working on the VTOL-capable Mirage IIIV and swing-wing Mirage G. Neither of these programmes would result in full series production but aspects of them would inform Dassault's ongoing fighter development.

The Mirage IIIF2 01 prototype, powered by a TF30 engine, made its first flight on June 12, 1966, with Jean Coureau at the controls. However, a month earlier France had withdrawn from NATO and the French general staff decided that a replacement for the earlier Mirage IIIs was needed. This aircraft would be an interceptor but with a secondary penetration role.

Dassault started work on a SNECMA/Pratt & Whitney TF306-engined development of the Mirage IIIF2 dubbed simply Mirage F3 but this was cancelled, according to Dassault itself, due to "another change in the definition of priorities by the Air Force and due to the success of programmes for variable geometry aircraft. It was also considered too costly and too dependent on American technology as regards the engine".

A Mirage III replacement was still needed though – so Dassault returned

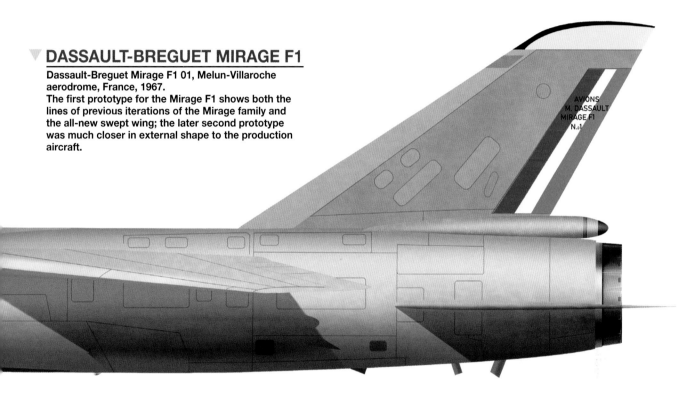

DASSAULT-BREGUET MIRAGE F1

Dassault-Breguet Mirage F1 01, Melun-Villaroche aerodrome, France, 1967.
The first prototype for the Mirage F1 shows both the lines of previous iterations of the Mirage family and the all-new swept wing; the later second prototype was much closer in external shape to the production aircraft.

DASSAULT-BREGUET MIRAGE F1C

Dassault-Breguet Mirage F1C, 30-MO/43, Escadron de Chasse 2/30 Normandie-Niémen, Armée de l'Air (Fighter Squadron 2/30, French Air Force), 112 air base, Reims-Champagne, France, 1986.
This aircraft from the famous Normandie-Niemen squadron carries the early Matra Magic and Matra 530 air-to-air missiles.

▼ DASSAULT-BREGUET MIRAGE F1C

Dassault-Breguet Mirage F1C-200, 30-LA/201, Escadron de Chasse 4/30 Vexin, Escadrille de Reconnaissance et Chasse 4/561 Mousquetaire bleu, Armée de l'Air (Fighter Squadron 4/30, Reconnaissance-Fighter Flight 4/561, French Air Force), 188 air base, Djibouti, 1993.
Deployed to Djibouti, this Mirage is painted in a fitting colour scheme; it carries Matra Magic training rounds on the wing tips with rocket pods and a Phimat chaff dispenser under the wings.

▼ DASSAULT-BREGUET MIRAGE F1CR

Dassault-Breguet Mirage F1CR, 33-NG/608, Escadron de reconnaissance 2/33 Savoie, Armé de l'Air (Reconnaissance Squadron 2/33, French Air Force), 112 air base, Reims-Champagne, France, 2003.
Painted with elements of the escadrille's emblems over the Savoie flag, this F1CR carries the Thales ASTAC ELINT pod.

DASSAULT-BREGUET MIRAGE F1AZ

Dassault-Breguet Mirage F1AZ, TR-KML/239, Escadron de chasse 1-02 Leyou, Armée de l'air Gabonaise (Fighter Squadron 1-02, Gabon Air Force), air base 02, Franceville, Gabon, 2005.
Gabon acquired its F1s from South Africa; this aircraft retained the former operator's camouflage scheme and has Gabonese civilian aviation registrations alongside the military serial number.

to the Mirage IIIE2 single-seater and redesignated it Mirage F1. This design was then built as a company-funded prototype powered by an interim SNECMA 9K 31 engine and was first flown, by René Bigand, on December 23, 1966. During the aircraft's fourth flight, on January 7, 1967, he reached Mach 2.

Bigand was killed on May 18, 1967, when the Mirage F1 01's tailplanes broke away due to flutter but the programme continued with an order for three further prototypes being placed by the government in September 1967. The first of these made its flight debut on March 20, 1968, flown by Jean-Marie Saget. The second, powered by a SNECMA Atar 9K 50, flew on September 18, 1969, and the third (the 04 prototype) on June 17, 1970.

By now, an order had been placed for a full production variant, to be known as the Mirage F1C, with the C standing for Chasseur or 'fighter' though it also had ground-attack capability. The first examples were delivered to the French Air Force on March 14, 1974.

The Atar 9K 50-powered F1C full production model was made using advanced honeycomb sandwich construction from aluminium alloy as well as steel and titanium. Internal fuel tanks were arranged around the engine bay and in the twin-spar swept wings. The tail had all-moving tailplanes, two fixed ventral fins and a brake parachute. Under the engine intakes were twin airbrakes.

The undercarriage had dual wheels all round, providing good rough-field capability. Inside the cockpit was a licence-made Martin-Baker Mk4 ejection seat and systems included TACAN beacon-navigation system, radar altimeter, datalink for ground-controlled interceptions, instrument landing system, VHF-UHF radio, IFF and Cyrano IV radar. Thomson-CSF RWR was fitted from the 71st example and from the 84th an 8cm fuselage 'plug' was added in front of the cockpit to allow the installation of a removable fixed refuelling probe offset to the right. Aircraft with this feature were designated F1C-200.

Armament was two DEFA 30mm cannon firing from the belly and wingtip AAM rails capable of carrying Matra 550 Magics. There were three stores stations able to carry a total of 4,000kg – one on the centreline and one under each wing; any of these could be used for drop tanks and multiple ejector racks could also be fitted to let each position carry more than one item. Options included a Barax or Barracuda jammer pod, long-range AAMs such as the Matra 530 or Super 530, SNEB 68mm rocket pods, iron bombs, Belouga cluster bombs, Durandal anti-runway bombs, BAP 120 anti-armour bombs and AS-37 ARMAT anti-radar missiles. A laser targeting pod could be installed on the centreline station, allowing the aircraft to carry AS-30L laser guided missiles.

FRENCH COMBAT JETS | Dassault Mirage F1

▼ DASSAULT-BREGUET MIRAGE F1BQ

Dassault-Breguet Mirage F1BQ, 3-6403, 102nd Tactical Fighter Squadron, Islamic Republic of Iran Air Force, 10th Tactical air base, Chahbahar, Iran, 2013.
Iran's Mirage F1s were former Iraqi aircraft that escaped over the border during the 1991 Gulf War; the aircraft have a new grey-blue colour scheme.

▼ DASSAULT-BREGUET MIRAGE F1EM-VI

Dassault-Breguet Mirage F1EM-VI, 170, Escadron de Chasse 'Atlas' (Fighter Squadron Atlas), Royal Moroccan Air Force, Sidi Slimane air base, Morocco, 2016.
Moroccan Mirages were used operationally in the West-Saharan conflict. Some of the fleet was upgraded to MF2000 standard starting in 2005, featuring improvements to radar, engine, avionics and weapons capabilities; this aircraft carries Matra MICA and Magic air-to-air missiles.

DASSAULT-BREGUET MIRAGE F1ED

Dassault-Breguet Mirage F1ED, 502, Libyan Air Force, Malta International Airport, Malta, 2011.
This is one of two Libyan Mirage F1s flown to Malta in 2011, their pilots claiming asylum. It is seen here at the Malta international Air show of that year with new national markings applied.

The centre station could also be fitted with a reconnaissance pod such as the RP-35P and a Phimat chaff/flare dispenser could be carried or a Lacroix dispenser could be carried in place of the brake chute in the tail instead.

The F1 proved to be more manoeuvrable than the Mirage III, with a 30% shorter take-off run and 25% lower approach speed. It had 43% more internal fuel capacity and 2.5 tonnes greater maximum take-off weight. A total of 162 F1Cs were bought.

There would also be 20 two-seater Mirage F1B trainers and 64 Mirage F1CR reconnaissance aircraft – the first of the latter entering service in 1983. The former had a 30cm longer fuselage to accommodate tandem Martin-Baker Mk10 seats, each under its own canopy, reduced fuel capacity and no internal cannon. It also lacked inflight refuelling but was combat capable.

The Mirage F1CR did have a refuelling probe as well as Mk.10 seats. It also had the enhanced Cyrano IVMR radar system. The nose held a vertical camera and a SAT SCM2400 Super Cyclope infrared linescan imager was installed in the bottom of the right engine nacelle – the space being freed up with the removal of one DEFA cannon. On many occasions the F1CR also carried a Thomson-CSF RAPHAEL-TH side-looking airborne radar pod on the centreline station which was capable of relaying real-time data to a ground station.

Three further F1 variants were offered to export customers the F1A, F1E and F1D. The simplified F1A had a lightweight Dassault Electronique Aida II radar, retractable refuelling probe and clear-weather ground-attack system integrating a Thomson-CSF TMV-630 laser rangefinder. The F1E was very similar to the F1C except it had the F1CR's Cyrano IVMR radar fitted. The F1D was effectively an F1B two-seater but with Cyrano IVMR.

The French Air Force retired its F1s in 2014 and 63 of them were sold to US firm ATAC in 2017 for use as aggressors.

SOUTH AFRICA

Having been one of the earliest adopters of the Mirage III, South Africa was keen to purchase France's next export fighter and as such signed a deal to manufacture 100 F1s and their engines locally. However, it soon became clear to the South Africans that the UN was preparing to impose an international arms embargo on them and as such they went for a purchase option instead – buying 32 F1AZs, effectively the stripped-back F1A model, and 16 F1CZs, based on the standard F1C. These were delivered from 1974 to 1975 with the embargo being imposed from November 1977.

These aircraft were flown in combat during the Border War and shot down a number of Angolan MiG-21s during the early 1980s. A South African F1AZ was lost to an SA-13 SAM on February 20, 1988, while flying over Angola. Seven

▼ DASSAULT-BREGUET MIRAGE F1JA

Dassault-Breguet Mirage F1JA, FAE-807, Escuadrón de Combate 2112, Ala de Combate 21, Fuerza Aérea Ecuatoriana (Combat squadron 2112, Combat Wing 21, Equatorian Air Force), Taura air base Ecuador, 2006.
This Mirage has a kill mark painted on the nose, representing the downing of a Peruvian Sukhoi Su-22 during the 1995 conflict; it carries Matra Magic 2 and Rafael Python 3 AAMs.

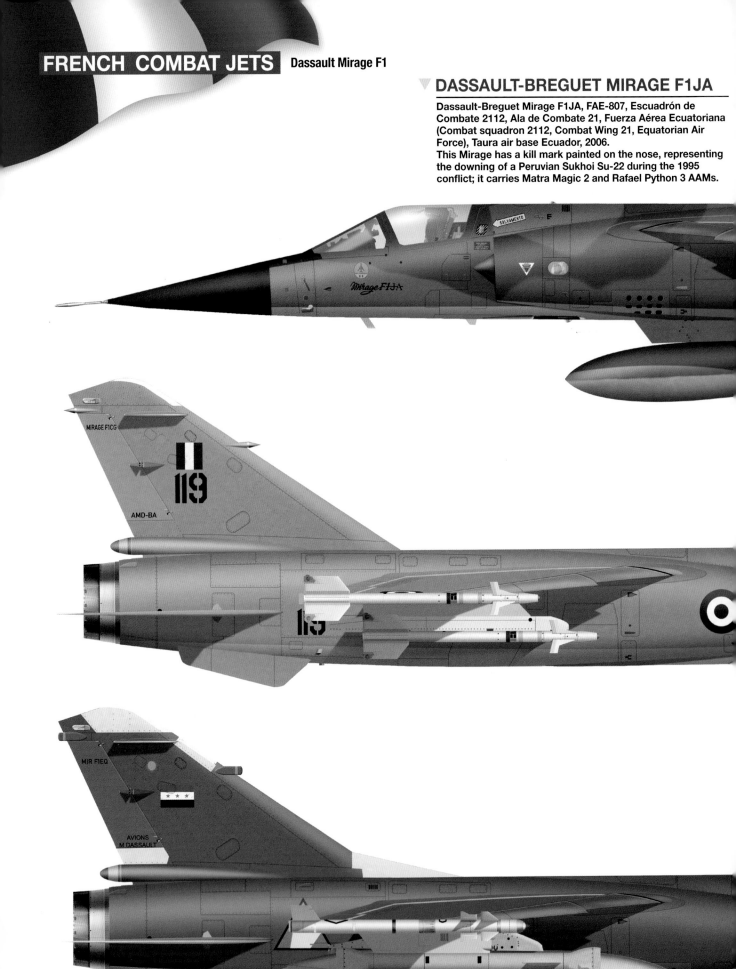

DASSAULT-BREGUET MIRAGE F1CG

Dassault-Breguet Mirage F1CG, 119, 342 MPK, 114 Ptéryga Máchis, Polemikí Aeroporía (342 all-weather squadron, 114 Combat Wing, Hellenic Air Force), Tanagra air base, Greece, 2000.
Greek Mirages were operated from 1975 until 2003; this aircraft carries AIM-9P air-to-air missiles.

DASSAULT-BREGUET MIRAGE F1EQ-6

Dassault-Breguet Mirage F1EQ-6, 4651, Iraq Air Force, Iraq, 1987.
Mirage F1EQ-5s and F1EQ-6s were capable of using the Exocet anti-ship missile, giving Iraq a major advantage in the so-called tanker war with Iran; besides the Exocet, this aircraft has Matra Magic missiles and Remora ECM pods.

others were destroyed as a result of mechanical failure or in accidents. One F1CZ was lost to enemy action and three more in accidents. The remaining F1CZs were retired in 1993 with the F1AZs following in 1997. Twenty-two of the remaining 24 F1AZs were offered for sale that same year and South African engineering firm Aerosud bought them in 2002. Six were refurbished and sold to the Gabonese Air Force in 2006-2007. In 2014 Aerosud Aerospace was renamed Paramount Aerospace and today offers private fighter pilot training using refurbished F1s.

SPAIN

A batch of 15 Mirage F1CEs were ordered by Spain in 1974 and the first three were delivered on June 18, 1975. A second set of ten F1CEs were then ordered in 1977 and delivered between June 1978 and May 1979. A third batch, this time consisting of 20 F1CEs, 22 F1EEs and six two-seater F1BEs, was ordered in 1978 and delivered from 1980 to March 1983 – giving Spain a fleet of 73 examples overall. The F1CEs were operated as interceptors and the F1EEs were used for ground-attack.

Starting in 1994, Spain bought 11 Qatari F1EDAs and two F1DDAs from Dassault to use for spares; it also bought four airworthy ex-French Air Force F1Cs and one F1B. Two of the Qatari airframes were sold on to Jordan in 1995. From 1996 to 2001, 48 of Spain's single-seaters and four of the two-seaters were upgraded to F1M standard by Thomson-CSF, subcontracted to EADS/CASA. The F1M featured a modernised cockpit configuration, new communications systems, upgraded navigational systems and updates allowing a wider range of weapons to be carried.

On January 20, 2009, two Spanish F1s collided in mid-air resulting in the deaths of three crew. By the end of that year there were 38 F1Ms still operational in Spanish service. The whole fleet was then retired in 2013 with 22 F1Ms then being sold to American firm Draken International for refurbishment and use in adversarial training.

GREECE

The Greek government order 40 F1CGs in 1974 and the first one – Greece's first ever French-made fighter – arrived on August 4, 1975. They were notable for being equipped to carry up to four American-made AIM-9P Sidewinders rather than the aircraft's usual Matra AAMs. An F1CG crashed near the island of Agios Efstratios in the Northern Aegean on June 18, 1992, with the death of the pilot, following a low-altitude encounter with two Turkish F-16s. And on February 8, 1995, a Turkish F-16C crashed into the sea after being intercepted by a Greek Mirage F1CG. The pilot bailed out and was rescued by a Greek helicopter. All 40 F1CGs were retired on June 30, 2003.

▼ DASSAULT-BREGUET MIRAGE F1EJ

Dassault-Breguet Mirage F1EJ, 110, 1 Squadron, Royal Jordanian Air Force, Muwaffaq Salti Air Base, Jordan, 1989. Jordanian Mirages operated alongside Northrop F-5s; the aircraft were acquired both in the C and E variants (along with a few examples of the two-seater B variant).

▷ DASSAULT-BREGUET MIRAGE F1CK

Dassault-Breguet Mirage F1CK, 710, Kuwait Air Force, Al Ahsa airport, Saudi Arabia, 1990. This Mirage has the Free Kuwait slogan that Kuwaiti aircraft displayed following the Iraqi invasion; it is armed with Matra Magic and Super 530 AAMs.

▷ DASSAULT-BREGUET MIRAGE F1EDA

Dassault-Breguet Mirage F1EDA, G, 7th Squadron, Qatar Emiri Air Force, Doha, Qatar, 1991. During Operation Desert Storm, Qatari Mirages operated from their own bases, performing ground-attack missions.

KUWAIT

The F1 was chosen as Kuwait's new air defence fighter in 1974 and an order was placed for 27 F1CK multirole single-seaters based on the F1E plus six F1BK two-seaters – a total of 33 – with deliveries in several batches between 1977 and 1983. When Iraq invaded Kuwait on August 2, 1990, the Kuwaiti Air Force was quickly overwhelmed but even so, Kuwaiti F1CK pilots claimed a total of 21 kills – 13 Mi-8 type helicopters, a pair of Aérospatiale Gazelle helicopters, two Mi-24 attack helicopters, one MiG-21, one Il-76 transport and two Su-22M4 swing-wing ground-attack aircraft. A number of Kuwaiti F1s were reportedly destroyed during the invasion but at least 15 survived. None are known to have been lost in combat. The Kuwaiti fleet was retired shortly after the Gulf War.

MOROCCO

Thirty F1CHs were ordered for the Royal Moroccan Air Force in 1975 with deliveries taking place from 1977 to December 1979. Although they were ostensibly interceptors, Morocco used them almost exclusively in the ground-attack role against rebel Polisario Front forces from 1979 up to the ceasefire in 1991. Twenty multirole F1EHs, six of them fitted with refuelling probes, were delivered from December 1979 to July 1982. In 2005, a programme of upgrades commenced to bring the Moroccan F1 fleet up to MF2000 standard with Thales RC400 (RDY-3) radar, engine modifications for improved thrust, modernised cockpits with multifunction displays, HUD and HOTAS controls, GPS navigation, night-vision goggles, new ejection seats and new electronics. A Moroccan F1 was lost to a bird strike on August 16, 2015 and another crashed due to a technical problem on January 21, 2019. Today Morocco reportedly continues to operate 46 F1s.

LIBYA

A total of 38 F1s were ordered for Libya in 1975 – 16 F1AD day fighters, 16 F1ED multirole aircraft and six F1DD two-seaters. All were delivered between 1978 and 1979 but Libya's involvement in the Chadian-Libyan War from 1978 to 1987 led to confrontation with France, Chad's former colonial power, and a cessation of spares. Eventually only around 14 were airworthy. By 2005, relations with France had improved and a programme of refurbishment and upgrade was planned for 12 F1s. However, only four had been completed when the First Libyan Civil War began in 2011.

On February 21, 2011, two Libyan pilots who had been ordered to bomb protesters in Benghazi landed their F1s in Malta and claimed political asylum. Another F1 was then shot down by rebel forces on March 2, 2011, leaving just a single F1DD trainer. The two 'defecting' aircraft flew back to Okba Ben Nafi air base near Tripoli in February 2012, a year to the day after they left. One Libyan F1 was then lost in June 2016 when a fuel pump failure caused it to crash. In May 2019, another F1, reportedly flown by a 29-year-old Portuguese mercenary, was shot down by a Libyan warlord. Two Libyan F1s were seen in flight in June 2021 and today it is believed that all remaining Libyan F1 airframes are in the hands of the Government of National Accord.

IRAQ

An order for 18 F1EQs was placed in 1977, with the first examples arriving in 1978. By 1988, Iraq had 93 F1EQs and 15 F1BQ two-seaters. The last 38 F1EQs were capable of carrying the AM39 Exocet. Another 25 F1s were on order but were not delivered because Iraq was unable to pay for them. During the Iran-Iraq War, Iraqi F1s are believed to have shot down around 35 Iranian F-4s and F-5E Tiger IIs – even an F-14 Tomcat being claimed on November 22, 1982.

▽ DASSAULT-BREGUET MIRAGE F1CZ

Dassault-Breguet Mirage F1CZ, 212, No. 3 squadron, South African Air Force, Waterkloof, South Africa, 1982.
South African F1s were heavily involved in the Border War, claiming several air kills against Angolan MiGs (flown by Cuban personnel); the SAAF also operated the F1AZ variant optimised for air-to-ground missions.

▽ DASSAULT-BREGUET MIRAGE F1M

Dassault-Breguet Mirage F1M, 14-37/C-14-64, Escuadrón 142, Ala 14, Ejército del Aire (Squadron 142, Wing 14, Spanish Air Force), Albacete air base, Los Llanos, Spain, 2006.
The Spanish Air Force presented this tiger-striped Mirage F1 at the 2006 NATO Tiger Meet. Mirage F1Ms were upgraded F1CE/EE aircraft featuring new cockpit interiors, avionics and upgraded radar.

Seven F1s were lost in combat. Iraqi F1EQs hit US Navy frigate *Stark* with two Exocets in a case of mistaken identity on May 17, 1987 – Iraq later apologising.

During the Gulf War in 1991, 23 F1EQs were destroyed with a further six suffering heavy damage. Twenty-four fled to Iran where they were seized.

ECUADOR
Nineteen F1s were ordered by Ecuador – 16 F1JA multirole fighters, based on the F1E, plus three F1JE two-seaters – and deliveries were made from 1978 to 1980. F1JAs carried out combat patrols during a border clash with Peruvian forces in early 1981, with one of them firing a

Magic missile at a Peruvian Su-22 but missing. A programme of upgrades was carried out with Israeli assistance during the late 1980s and early 1990s and in 1995, during another border skirmish with Peru, F1JAs claimed to have shot down two Su-22Ms. The Peruvians denied it. The Ecuadorian fleet was retired in 2011.

QATAR
Seeking to modernise its air force in 1979, Qatar ordered 13 F1EDA multirole fighters and two F1DDA two-seaters. Deliveries took place between 1980 and 1984 and the aircraft played a limited role during the Gulf War, flying only when accompanied by F-16s and only

on ground-attack missions, to avoid confusion with Iraqi F1s. Most Qatari F1s were sold to Spain for spare parts, starting in 1994.

JORDAN
A total of 35 F1s were bought for Jordan by Saudi Arabia and delivered from 1981 to 1983 – 17 F1CJ interceptors, 17 F1EJ multirole fighters and a pair of F1BJ two-seaters. An F1CJ was destroyed in

a crash on February 18, 1985, when a technical failure led to a sudden loss of control. The pilot was killed.

Jordan acquired two ex-Qatari F1DDAs from Spain in 1995 and brought them into service as F1DJs. A second Jordanian F1CJ was lost to a technical

failure during a routine training mission on October 19, 2003. The pilot of this aircraft was also killed.

Two further F1s were acquired from Spain in 2006 and the RJAF retired all remaining F1s in 2010, putting them into storage. Twenty-five were then sold to

▼ DASSAULT-BREGUET MIRAGE F1M

Dassault-Breguet Mirage F1M, N576EM/576, Draken International, Nellis Air Force Base, USA, 2021.
Ex-Spanish Mirage F1M operated by Draken International, displaying digital camouflage colours as it performs dissimilar air combat training from Nellis Air Force base.

▼ DASSAULT-BREGUET MIRAGE F1B

Dassault-Breguet Mirage F1B, Escadron de Chasse 1/30 Alsace, Armée de l'Air (Fighter Squadron 1/30, French Air Force), 132 air base, Colmar-Meyenheim, France, 2006.
For the 65th anniversary of the squadron, one of its two-seaters was painted in this stunning colour scheme.

American company Draken International in April 2020. All 25 were registered with the FAA in October 2022.

IRAN
Twenty-four Iraqi Mirage F1s were captured by Iran when they landed at Iranian air bases seeking safe harbour during the Gulf War in 1991. Without spares or expert servicing, most of these aircraft quickly became unusable but a refurbishment and upgrade programme aimed at putting them into service, Project Habibi, began 16 years later in 2007. This encompassed a dozen airframes which continue in Iranian service today.

GABON
The Gabonese purchased six ex-South African F1AZs from Aerosud in 2005-2007 and they remain in service today with ongoing support from Aerosud, now known as the Paramount Group.

CONGO
A pair of ex-South African F1AZs were also sold to the Democratic Republic of Congo in 2011 by Paramount. They remain in service.

SEPECAT JAGUAR

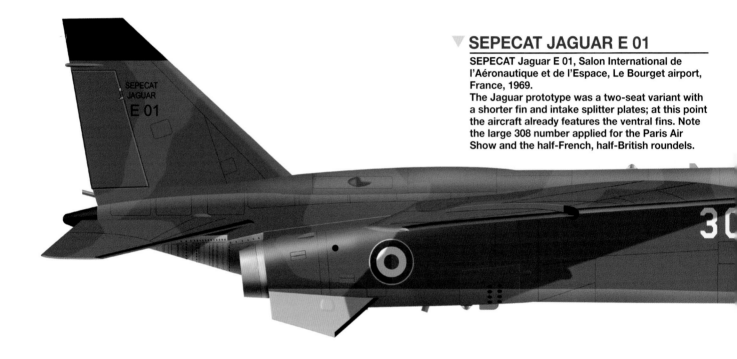

▼ SEPECAT JAGUAR E 01

SEPECAT Jaguar E 01, Salon International de l'Aéronautique et de l'Espace, Le Bourget airport, France, 1969.

The Jaguar prototype was a two-seat variant with a shorter fin and intake splitter plates; at this point the aircraft already features the ventral fins. Note the large 308 number applied for the Paris Air Show and the half-French, half-British roundels.

▼ SEPECAT JAGUAR A

SEPECAT Jaguar A, 11-MH/A117, Escadron de Chasse 2/11 Vosges, Escadrille SPA 97 – Fanion aux hermines, Armée de l'Air (Fighter Squadron 2/11, Flight SPA 97, French Air force), 136 air base, Toul-Rosières, France, 1990.

French Air Force Jaguars also performed electronic warfare missions; this one carries Caiman and Barracuda electronic countermeasures pods.

1973-NOW

Standing alongside Concorde as an example of what Anglo-French cooperation can achieve, SEPECAT's quick and agile Jaguar has proven to be an excellent multirole aircraft.

Both France and Britain issued requirements during the early 1960s for a new jet trainer to replace their existing Fouga Magisters and Hunters/Gnats respectively.

Designs were tendered to the French requirement by Breguet, Potez, Sud-Aviation, Nord and Dassault, while BAC, Hunting, Hawker Siddeley and Folland tendered for the British requirement. It was eventually realised, however, that these requirements were very similar and in the spirit of cross-channel cooperation that would lead to Concorde and the Gazelle, a joint requirement was issued in March 1964.

This was refined seven months later and a memorandum of understanding

signed on May 17, 1965. The new trainer, it was decided, would need to be capable of performing the light strike mission and would also need to provide the basis of a more advanced ground-attack aircraft with variable geometry wings (known as Anglo-French Variable Geometry or AFVG). The name 'Jaguar' was announced in June 1965.

Each nation agreed to buy 150 examples; the French would take 75 two-seater trainers (Jaguar E for Ecole) and 75 of the attack variant (Jaguar A for Appui) while Britain's 150 would all be two-seater trainers (Jaguar B for Biplace).

A new company was formed in May 1966 by Breguet and BAC to make the Jaguar E and B – Société Européenne de

Production de l'Avion d'École de Combat et d'Appui Tactique, aka SEPECAT. Meanwhile, Dassault and BAC would make the Jaguar A.

During initial development, the British pushed increased capability for the Jaguar E and B, changing the specification to create a larger and more powerful aircraft. AFVG was cancelled in June 1967 and on January 9, 1968, the French and British governments signed another memorandum of understanding on Jaguar – agreeing to buy 200 aircraft each. France now wanted 85 Jaguar Es and 75 Jaguar As, plus 40 carrier-capable Jaguar M (for Marine) strike fighters for the Aeronavale. Britain

▼ SEPECAT JAGUAR A

SEPECAT Jaguar A, 7-IF/A61, Escadron de Chasse 3/7 'Languedoc', Escadrille SPA 38 'Chardon lorrain', Armée de l'Air (Fighter Squadron 3/7, Flight SPA 38, French Air Force), 113 air base, Saint-Dizier-Robinson, France, 1985.
This Jaguar carries an AN-52 bomb in the nuclear strike role.

▶ SEPECAT JAGUAR A

SEPECAT Jaguar A, 3-XJ/A16, Escadron de Chasse 3/3 Ardennes, Armée de l'Air (Fighter Squadron 3/3, French Air Force), Chad, 1987.
During Operátion Epervier, Jaguars from the EC 3/3 performed an attack against Libyan forces in Chad, using the AS.37 Martel anti-radiation missile to destroy SAM installations.

▶ SEPECAT JAGUAR E

SEPECAT Jaguar E, 7-PC/E22, Escadron Chasse 2/7 argone, Escadrille SPA 31 – Archer grec, Armée de l'Air (Fighter Squadron 2/7, Flight SPA 31, French Air Force), France, 1994.
EC 2/7 was the operational conversion unit for the French Jaguar fleet; French two-seaters had a fixed inflight refuelling probe on the nose.

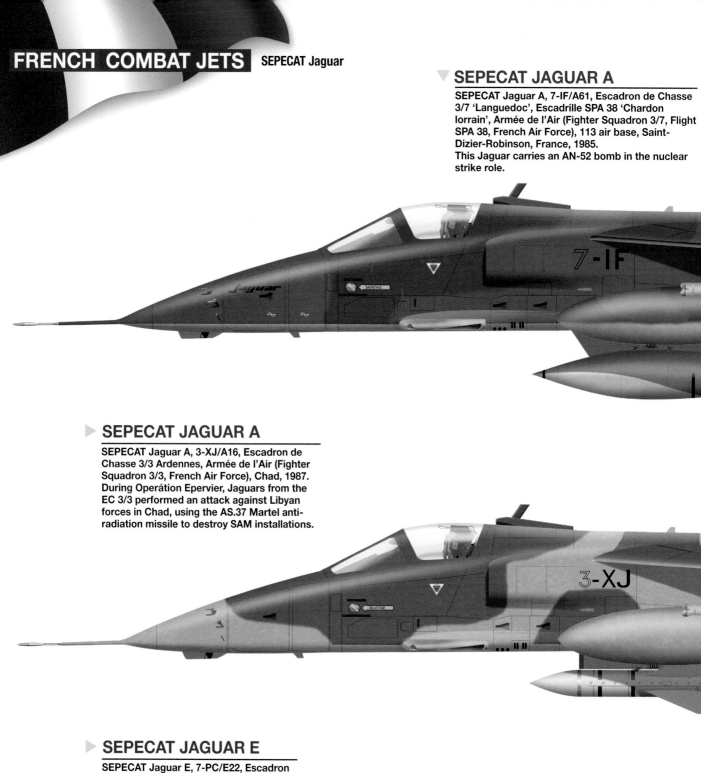

would take 110 Jaguar B trainers plus 90 Jaguar S (for Strike) strike fighters.

The first French Jaguar E trainer prototype flew on September 8, 1968, followed by the first Jaguar A attack aircraft on March 23, 1969. The lone Jaguar M prototype, with longer nosewheel leg, arrestor hook and other navy-specific features first flew on November 14, 1969. The latter completed deck trials but was cancelled in favour of Dassault's Super Étendard.

Meanwhile, Britain's first Jaguar S made its flight debut on October 12, 1969, eventually followed by the first Jaguar B on August 30, 1971, the British having meanwhile amended their order again to 165 Jaguar S and just 35 Jaguar B.

The Jaguar A single-seater had a conventional configuration with shoulder-mounted 40-degree swept wings that had an anhedral droop of three-degrees. Rather than ailerons, roll control was via two-section wingtop spoilers positioned slightly forward of the outboard flaps. There was also a prominent fence between the inboard and outboard wing sections.

The tail was also relatively conventional with all-moving tailplanes and two ventral fins. Ahead of those fins, under the wings, were two hydraulically-actuated perforated airbrakes.

Power was initially provided by two afterburning Adour 101s, these soon being replaced by the modified Adour 102. The engines' intakes were mounted high up to prevent ingestion of foreign objects during rough field operations and the Jaguar A had five internal fuel tanks.

The undercarriage, with single nosewheel and twin-wheel main gear, was fitted with low pressure tyres and was ruggedly constructed, again for rough-field use. A runway arrestor hook was installed between the engine exhausts and there was a brake parachute in the tailcone which could be swapped out for a countermeasures dispenser.

The air-conditioned and pressurised cockpit featured a Martin-Baker Mk4 seat and armoured windscreen. There was a Decca Doppler navigation radar, HUD, IFF, RWR and fire-control system. Initially an OMERA 40 panoramic camera was installed in a fairing under the nose but midway through production this was replaced with a TAV38 laser rangefinder.

Armament was two DEFA 553 cannon in the fuselage behind the cockpit, plus two pylons under each wing and one centreline position capable of taking a combined total of 4,540kg of stores. The centreline and inner wing pylons had piping for external fuel tanks and a retractable refuelling probe was fitted on the right hand side of the nose.

A typical load might include iron bombs, Belouga or other cluster munitions, unguided rocket pods, Matra Magic missiles or Martel anti-radar missiles. Late production Jaguar As carried an ATLIS laser target-designator pod on the centreline position for BGL bombs and AS-30L missiles. Alternatively, an RP63P reconnaissance pod could be carried. The Jaguar A could, if required, also carry the AN-52 nuclear bomb.

The Jaguar E two-seater was 70cm longer than the Jaguar A. It had the same engines but reduced avionics and no retractable refuelling probe – though

some carried a fixed probe. The rear seat was 38cm higher than the front seat to give the back-seater a better view.

In the end, France bought 160 Jaguar As and two Jaguar Es for the French Air Force. They were first flown into combat in December 1977 against Polisario rebels fighting the Mauritanian government, then they carried out strikes against Libyan-backed insurgents in Chad in 1978. In February 1986 they deployed anti-runway munitions at an air

▼ SEPECAT JAGUAR M

SEPECAT Jaguar M, M.05, Society of British Aircraft Constructors air show, Farnborough, UK, 1970.
The Jaguar M programme was intended to provide the Aéronavale with a replacement for its Étendard jets but the aircraft was not selected, Dassault's Super Étendard being the preferred choice. This aircraft has the Royal Aircraft Establishment (RAE) crest on the splitter plate and testing markings denoting cable hook arrest and catapult launches on the front fuselage, since it was tested both at the RAE's facilities and on the aircraft carrier *Clemenceau*. This view shows the arrestor hook deployed.

base built by the Libyans at Ouadi Doum in northern Chad – causing massive damage. Jaguars hit the base again in January 1987, knocking out its radar stations. During Desert Storm, French Jaguars flew more than 600 combat sorties, striking ground targets with AS-30L missiles.

All French Jaguars had been retired by 2001.

BRITAIN
The Jaguar S became the Jaguar GR.1 in RAF service, while the Jaguar B became the Jaguar T.2. The British models were largely similar to their French counterparts but came with a Ferranti/Marconi NAVWASS navigation and weapon arming subsystem as well as a Plessey 10-way weapon control system. Some were capable of carrying the WE.177 bomb in the nuclear strike role.

Starting in December 1983, 75 Jaguar GR.1s and 14 T.2s were upgraded to GR.1A and T.2A standard respectively, with FIN1064 nav/attack systems replacing the original Ferranti/Marconi system. Most were also re-engined with the Adour 104 and were given the ability to carry AIM-9 Sidewinders or AN-ALQ-101(V)-10 electronic countermeasures pods on their underwing pylons.

In 1990, RAF Jaguars were fitted with optional overwing pylons which could be used to carry Sidewinders. Britain sent 12 Jaguar GR.1As to participate in the Gulf War and they flew 612 combat sorties against ground targets. In 1994, ten GR.1As and two T.2As were upgraded to GR.1B and T.2B standard respectively, which allowed them to carry the TIALD laser target-designator pod. These aircraft were deployed

▼ SEPECAT JAGUAR A

SEPECAT Jaguar A, 11-RW/A158, Escadron de Chasse 3/11 Corse, Escadrille SPA 88 Serpent, Armée de l'Air (Fighter Squadron 3/ 11, Flight SPA 88, French Air Force), Al-Ahsa Airport, Saudi Arabia, 1991.
The French contribution to the liberation of Kuwait, Operation Daguet, saw the deployment of several Jaguars to Saudi Arabia. This aircraft carries a Matra Magic, an AS-30L laser-guided missile under the wing and an ATLIS laser designator pod on the centreline pylon; it shows the retractable air-refuelling probe.

SEPECAT JAGUAR IS

SEPECAT Jaguar IS, JS135, No. 5 Squadron 'Tuskers', Indian Air Force, Ambala Air Force Station, India, 1982.
The Indian Air Force is the largest export user of the Jaguar, with most of its aircraft having been produced under licence in India. Initially several aircraft were borrowed from the RAF, until newly built examples could be obtained.

SEPECAT JAGUAR SO

SEPECAT Jaguar International SO, 224, 20 Squadron, Royal Air Force of Oman, Thumrait air base, Oman, 2008.
Omani Jaguars were operated by two squadrons, No. 20 and No. 8; this aircraft carries AIM-9P Sidewinders.

SEPECAT JAGUAR A

SEPECAT Jaguar A, 7-NE, Escadron de Chasse 4/7 'Limousin d'Istres', Armée de l'Air (Fighter Squadron 4/7, French Air Force), 125 air base, Istres-Le Tubé, France, 1989.
This Jaguar was part of the Patrouille RAMEX demonstration team and had the 80-89 inscription applied on the occasion of the unit's dissolution.

to Italy that August to take part in Operation Deliberate Force against Bosnian Serb forces, designating targets for RAF Harriers.

Further upgrades were later carried out to bring the RAF's Jaguars up to GR.3 standard with a new HUD, new hand controller, integrated GPS and terrain referenced navigation; the two-seater equivalent was the T.4. This was followed by the GR.3A upgrade which included new Adour 106 turbofan engines, a helmet-mounted sight, datalink and night vision goggles.

Britain's Jaguar fleet was retired in April 2007.

ECUADOR

Dassault bought Breguet in 1971 and effectively handed development of the Jaguar over to BAC/British Aerospace, since it was a competitor for Dassault's own products. As a result, the export version of the Jaguar, the Jaguar International, was largely a British creation. The first prototype made its flight debut on September 2, 1975 and was based on the Jaguar GR.1/T.2. It was initially powered by the Adour 804, a modified version of the Adour 104. Avionics were down to customer preference but were usually based on RAF systems.

The Jaguar International could be optionally fitted with Agave radar, which allowed the aircraft to carry the British Aerospace Sea Eagle anti-ship missile on its centreline. Overwing launchers were offered, which could carry either the AIM-9 or Matra's Magic AAM.

Ecuador was an early adopter, ordering ten Jaguar ES single-seaters and two Jaguar EB two-seaters in 1974. Deliveries were then made in 1977. Three attrition replacements were supplied in 1991, all of them refurbished ex-RAF GR.1s. All Ecuadorian Jaguars were retired in 2003.

OMAN

Like Ecuador, Oman was quick to order the Jaguar International – the deal including ten Jaguar OS single-seaters and two Jaguar OB two-seaters. These were delivered from 1977 to 1978 and a second identical order for 12 followed in 1980, with deliveries being made in 1983. The two seaters in the second batch had French-style fixed refuelling probes and ARI 18223 RWR fitted. A single ex-RAF T.2 was delivered as a replacement in 1982, as was a GR.1 in 1986. The latter aircraft had been part of a batch loaned to India and was flown direct to Oman from there.

Twenty-one Omani Jaguars received the FIN 1064 nav/attack system upgrade from 1986 to 1989, effectively making them GR.1As. The whole Omani Jaguar fleet was stood down in 2014.

NIGERIA

An order for 18 Jaguars was placed by Nigeria in early 1983 – 13 Jaguar SN single-seaters and five Jaguar BN two-seaters. Deliveries commenced in 1984 but Nigeria was forced to withdraw its fleet in 1991 because it could no longer afford to keep them flying. They were then placed in storage. When they were finally put up for sale in 2007, it emerged than some airframes had as few as 150 hours on them. However, a feasibility study in 2009 found that only 16 of the aircraft had any hope of being resurrected and even then doing so would be prohibitively expensive. Another attempt to sell them in 2011 failed and as such Nigeria still has the aircraft in storage.

INDIA
After a 12 year long selection process for a successor to the Indian Air Force's Canberras and Hunters, which looked at

▽ SEPECAT JAGUAR BN

SEPECAT Jaguar International BN, NAF-700, Nigerian Air Force, Makurdi air base, Nigeria, 1986.
Nigerian Jaguars were only operated for about seven years, being retired from service in 1991.

▽ SEPECAT JAGUAR ES

SEPECAT Jaguar International ES, FAE-302, Escuadron de Combate 2111 'Águilas', Ala de combate 21, Fuerza Aérea Ecuatoriana (Combat Squadron 2112, Combat Wing 21, Ecuadorian Air Force), Taura air base, Ecuador, 2010.
Ecuadorian Jaguars saw combat during border conflicts with Peru; this aircraft carries Matra rocket pods and Magic 2 missiles.

both the Mirage F1 and SAAB Viggen, the Jaguar was finally chosen in October 1978. To get things started, the RAF loaded 16 GR.1s and a pair of T.2s to the Indian Air Force in 1979. Two of these would be lost in Indian service and the rest were returned during the early 1980s, one going to Oman.

The first batch of Indian Jaguars, made in Britain and delivered starting in 1981, consisted of 35 Jaguar IS single-seaters and five Jaguar IB two-seaters. The former was similar to the GR.1 with Adour 804E engines and the NAVWASS system. The latter was similar to the T.2. In Indian service, the Jaguar was known as the Shamser or 'Sword of Justice'.

The second batch of 45 single-seaters were assembled under licence in India by Hindustan Aeronautics Limited (HAL) from kits, the delivery of which also commenced in 1981. HAL then began to build 35 more aircraft itself including the Adour engines, with the first HAL-made Jaguar entering Indian Air Force service in 1985. These had Adour 811 engines and locally-made avionics systems known as DARIN (Display Attack Ranging Inertial Navigation). Ten single-seaters, designated Jaguar IM, were fitted with the Agave radar and carried Sea Eagle anti-ship missiles. India's Jaguars can carry reconnaissance pods and the type is also believed to be Indians' delivery platform for freefall nuclear weapons.

By 1999, the Indian Air Force had received a total of 120 Jaguars – the

initial 40 plus 80 assembled or built by HAL. Meanwhile, an order for 17 more Jaguar IB two-seaters had been placed with HAL in 1998 and deliveries began in 2003. These were configured for night attack, with the Israeli Rafael Litening

targeting pod. Then an order for another 20 single-seaters was placed in 2006, with deliveries from 2010 – taking the overall total received to 157.

These latter 37 aircraft were also fitted with DARIN II, which included

▼ SEPECAT JAGUAR IM

SEPECAT Jaguar International IM, JM-252, No. 6 Squadron 'Dragons', Indian Air Force, Jamnagar Air Force Station, India, 1990.
No. 6 Squadron has a maritime strike role, using Jaguar IM aircraft fitted with the CSF Agave radar and carrying the British Sea Eagle anti-ship missile (in this case a training round).

a new wide-angle HUD, SAGEM 95 navigation system with gyro INS and GPS receiver, a new LRMTS in a reprofiled nose, an Elta EL/L-8222 RF jammer replacing the right cannon, with the gun port being faired over, Indian-made Tarang RWR, licence-made IAI Malat countermeasures

dispenser, autopilot and mission computers.

A series of upgrades to DARIN III standard commenced in 2016, including a full 'glass cockpit' incorporating multifunction displays, digital HUD and helmet-mounted display, plus new mission computers,

data recorders, radar altimeter, autopilot, IFF and EL/M-2052 active-array radar replacing the LRMTS. In 2018, India bought 31 airframes from France plus two each from Britain and Oman to cannibalise for spares. The Indian Air Force currently operates around 130 Jaguars.

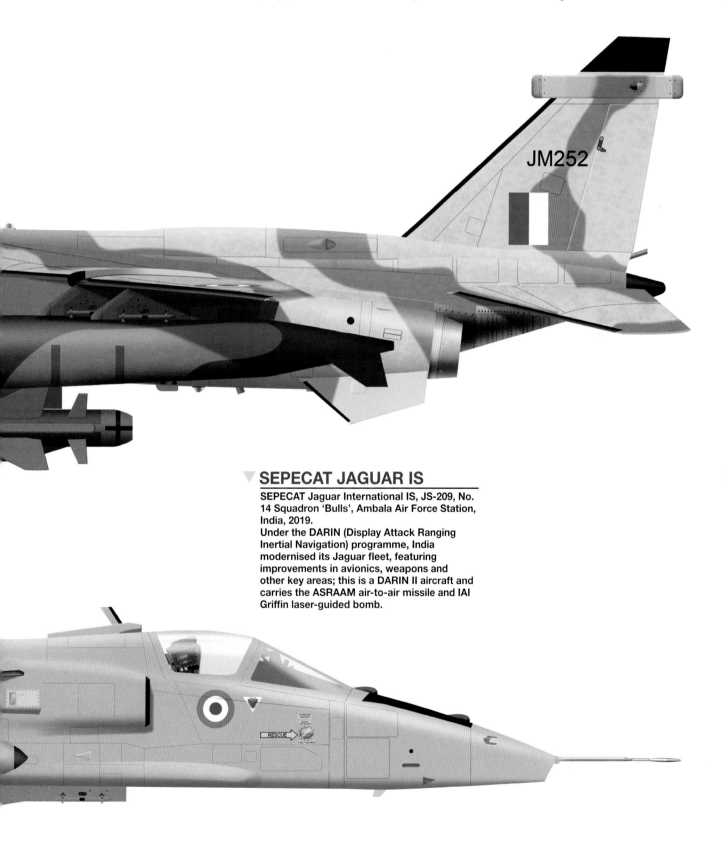

▼ SEPECAT JAGUAR IS

SEPECAT Jaguar International IS, JS-209, No. 14 Squadron 'Bulls', Ambala Air Force Station, India, 2019.
Under the DARIN (Display Attack Ranging Inertial Navigation) programme, India modernised its Jaguar fleet, featuring improvements in avionics, weapons and other key areas; this is a DARIN II aircraft and carries the ASRAAM air-to-air missile and IAI Griffin laser-guided bomb.

DASSAULT MIRAGE 2000

Dassault's delta legacy continues with the Mirage 2000 – a highly advanced multirole fighter to rival the American F-16 or the Russian MiG-29.

1984-NOW

The convoluted story of the Mirage 2000 began with Dassault's partnership with British firm BAC to produce the AFVG swing-wing fighter, associated with Jaguar, in 1965. This fell apart in 1967 when the French government backed a solo Dassault variable geometry project instead – Mirage G.

This led to the Mirage G4 in 1968, a twin-engine two-seater multirole version of the G. Two prototypes were ordered but these were instead built as the Mirage G8 interceptor. The French government decided against putting this into production and instead backed a new fixed-wing strike version known as the G8A or 'Avion de Combat Futur' aka ACF. The prototype for this design, which would have been a sort of French multirole F-15 equivalent, was reportedly almost complete when the French government cancelled it in 1975 due to its sheer cost – two and a half times as much as a Mirage F1.

Meanwhile, since 1972 Dassault had been working privately on various smaller, simpler and cheaper designs with the export market in mind. When ACF was cancelled, the company immediately offered one of these as an alternative – the Mirage 2000. Externally, it mostly retained the familiar size and shape of the Mirage III/5/50 but it was a completely new machine and incorporated critical technology developed for the ACF, particularly its SNECMA M53 afterburning turbofan engine, though it would only have one compared to the ACF's two.

The first of four single-seat Mirage 2000C (C for Chasseur or 'fighter') prototypes flew on March 10, 1978, piloted by Jean Coreau, and a lone two-seater 2000B (B for Biplane) prototype followed on October 11, 1980, flown by Michel Porta. Meanwhile, the French government decided that a two-seater Mirage 2000 would be their next nuclear

▼ DASSAULT-BREGUET MIRAGE 2000B

Dassault-Breguet Mirage 2000B, 2-FX/521, Escadron de Chasse 2/2 'Côte d'Or', SPA 94 'Mort qui fauche', Armée de l'Air (Fighter squadron 2/2, Flight 94, French Air Force), Air base 102, Dijon-Longvic, France, 1995.
The two-seat variant retained most of the combat capability of the single-seater, able to carry air-to-air missiles such as the depicted Matra Magic 2 and Super 530D as well as other weapons. It had no internal guns however, and internal fuel capacity was reduced.

▼ DASSAULT-BREGUET MIRAGE 2000 02

Dassault-Breguet Mirage 2000 02, Salon International de l'Aéronautique et de l'Espace, Le Bourget airport, France, 1979.
The second prototype for the Mirage 2000 is seen here painted in national colours at the 1979 Paris Air Show. The prototypes had a tall slender fin during early testing, before being retrofitted with the production one.

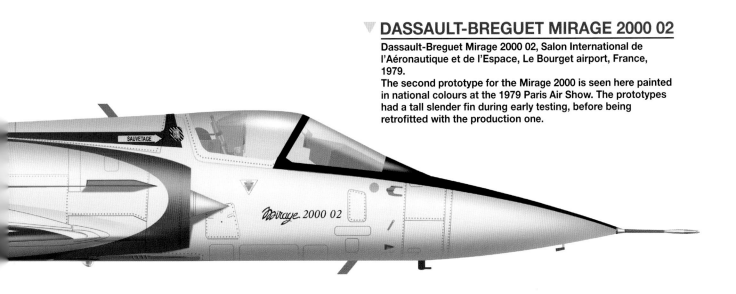

DASSAULT-BREGUET MIRAGE 2000C

Dassault-Breguet Mirage 2000C, 5-OP/74, Escadron de Chasse 2/5 Ile-de-France, Armée de l'Air (Fighter squadron 2/5, French Air Force), Al Ahsa airport, Saudi Arabia, 1991.
The French contribution for the liberation of Kuwait, known as Operation Daguet, saw the deployment of several combat squadrons to the region; EC 2/5 was the first French Air Force unit to do so. The aircraft had an appropriate desert camouflage colour scheme.

DASSAULT-BREGUET MIRAGE 2000D

Dassault-Breguet Mirage 2000D, 3-XN/652, Escadron de Chasse 3/3 'Ardennes', Armée de l'Air (Fighter squadron 3/3, French Air Force), Air base 133, Nancy-Ochey, France, 2017.
The Mirage 2000D is a two-seat dedicated conventional attack variant. This aircraft has a special paint scheme to commemorate the 30th anniversary of the raid against Libyan forces at Ouadi Doum in Chad.

DASSAULT-BREGUET MIRAGE 2000N

Dassault-Breguet Mirage 2000N, 4-BM/349, Escadron de Chasse 2/4 La Fayette, Escadrille N. 124 'Sioux', Armée de l'Air (Fighter squadron 2/4, Flight N.124, French Air Force), air base 125, Istres-Le Tubé, France, 2004.
The appropriately designated N variant had a nuclear strike role; depicted here is a Matra ASMP (Air-Sol Moyenne Mortée – medium-range air-to-surface) nuclear missile carried on the centreline pylon; the aircraft usually also carried external fuel tanks on the wing pylons and air-to-air missiles for self-defence.

delivery platform under the designation 2000P (P for Penetration). This was later changed to 2000N (N for Nucleaire) and the first of two prototypes, based on the 2000B, flew on February 3, 1983, with Porta at the controls.

The first production Mirage 2000C had flown on November 20, 1982, and the type then entered French service in 1984. Although it looked like the Mirage III, the centre of lift was shifted to the front of its centre of gravity, giving it a level of instability which improved manoeuvrability – lack of which had long been the Mirage III's most noticeable failing.

A fly-by-wire automatic flight control system compensated for the instability and each wing had two-piece elevons plus automatic full-length two-piece leading-edge slats and an airbrake on top. The tailfin was taller, allowing better control at high angles of attack.

The undercarriage had a dual nosewheel with single wheel main gear, fitted with beefy carbon brakes, and an arrestor hook or brake parachute fairing could be installed under the tail, though a Dassault Éclair countermeasures dispenser was usually carried there instead.

Built-in armament was two DEFA 554 30mm cannon and there were two pylons under each wing plus a further five under the fuselage for a total of nine, able to carry up to 6,300kg of stores between them. The centreline position and inner wing pylons could carry external fuel tanks and a refuelling probe could be fixed in front of the cockpit and to the right, if desired.

As an interceptor, the Mirage 2000C carried Matra Super 530 medium-range AAMs on the inboard wing pylons and Matra Magics on the outer positions. For attack, it might carry iron bombs, cluster bombs or Matra 68mm rocket pods.

The 2000C was fitted with M53-5 engines and carried a Thomson-CSF Radar Doppler Multifunction (RDM) system as well as a SAGEM ULISS 52 inertial nav system, air data computer, TACAN beacon nav system, ILS landing system, RWR and RF jammer pod under the tailfin. In the cockpit, the pilot sat on a licence-made Martin-Baker Mk10 seat and had mostly analogue instrumentation plus a head-down radar display and HUD.

The French Air Force got a total of 124 Mirage 2000Cs and from the 38th example they were fitted with uprated M53-P2 engines. In 1987, the RDM was replaced by the Radar Doppler Impulse (RDI) and the Éclair was replaced by a pair of Matra Spirale dispensers, one behind each wingroot. The 2000C was later armed with the improved Matra MICA AAM. The Mirage 2000B was very similar to the 2000C but without built-in cannon. The French Air Force acquired 30 examples.

The first of 75 production model Mirage 2000Ns flew on March 1986.

DASSAULT MIRAGE 2000-9

Dassault Mirage 2000-9, 759, United Arab Emirates
Air Force and Air Defence, Fighter Wing, Al Dhafra
Air Base, United Arab Emirates, 2018.
UAE's Mirages saw action on several instances,
including the Gulf War and, more recently, during
the Libya and Yemen conflicts; this aircraft carries
the Al-Tariq guided bomb and the Matra Magic 2
air-to-air missile.

DASSAULT-BREGUET MIRAGE 2000H

Dassault-Breguet Mirage 2000H Vajra, KF104, No. 7 Squadron
'Battle Axes', Indian Air Force, Gwalior air base, India, 1990.
No.7 Squadron was the first IAF unit to be equipped with
Mirage 2000s in 1985. Indian Mirages were used in operations
in Sri Lanka, Bangladesh and border clashes with Pakistan.
This aircraft has a unique brown/green camouflage scheme
and carries laser-guided bombs plus the Remora ECM pod.

DASSAULT MIRAGE 2000I

Dassault Mirage 2000I, KF-107, Hindustan Aeronautics Limited, Bangalore, India, 2015. India upgraded its Mirages starting in 2011; the new aircraft, designated 2000I (single seat) and 2000TI (dual-seat), features radar, avionics and weapons improvements. This aircraft was the first upgraded and is seen carrying Matra MICA air-to-air missiles.

Differences from the 2000B included strengthened wings and a low-level precision nav/attack system using the Dassault/Thales Antilope 5 radar. It also had improved defensive countermeasures including better ELINT capability and a SAT Samir missile-warning system.

It carried a single ASMP ramjet-powered Mach 3 nuclear cruise missile on its centreline pylon and could also carry AAMs for self-defence. The first 31 examples, designated 2000N-K1, could not carry any further stores, but the rest could also carry the usual array of strike munitions from iron bombs to rocket pods, or a twin cannon pod, and were designated 2000N-K2. In place of the ASMP, both 2000Ns could later carry the Reco NG reconnaissance pod. Thirty Mirage 2000Ns were updated from 2009 to carry the longer-ranged ASMP-A cruise missile and were redesignated Mirage 2000N-K3.

Back in 1986 it had been announced that due to delays in the Rafale programme, a new version of the Mirage 2000N would be produced that was dedicated to conventional attack. Development formally began in 1988 and the type was given the new designation Mirage 2000D (D for 'Diversifie' or multirole) in 1990. The first prototype was flown on February 19, 1991, and the first production model aircraft flew on March 31, 1993, with introduction to service taking place in April 1995.

The 2000D had a new cockpit layout with improved HOTAS controls and a second screen for the pilot up front while the back-seater got two more screens for a total of three. It also got a modernised ULISS 52P nav system, Antilope 50 terrain-following, ICMS 2 countermeasures system with SERVAL RWR, Chameleon jammer and Spirale dispensers, and upgrades to carry a wider array of weapons. The earlier 2000Ds were designated 2000D-R1, with a total of 86 being delivered by 2001. Then a programme of upgrades followed, taking the aircraft up to 2000D-R2 status with enhanced countermeasures and support for even more weapons and the Thales ASTAC ELINT pod on the centreline station.

Starting in 2017, Dassault began work on the 2000D RMV (rénovés à mi-vie) mid-life upgrade programme. This saw 55 French Air Force 2000D airframes upgraded to Mirage 2000D RMV standard with a focus on enabling the aircraft to carry and launch a huge variety of different air-to-ground weapons. The TALIOS targeting pod can also be carried. The first Mirage 2000D RMVs entered service in 2021.

Meanwhile, during the late 1980s Dassault and Thomson-CSF had worked together on an update of the Mirage 2000C known as the Mirage 2000-5, with the goal of competing with the F-16 in the export market. A two-seat prototype 2000-5 was first flown by Patrick Experton on October 24, 1990, and a single-seat Mirage 2000C was then brought up to 2000-5 standard and made its flight debut in this configuration on April 27, 1991.

While visually very difficult to distinguish from the 2000C, the 2000-5 lacked the nose pitot probe and internally it was hugely upgraded. It now carried Thales multimode RDY radar, improved computer systems, ICMS 2 countermeasures and a Rafale-style glass cockpit. The ability to carry larger drop tanks improved range and the 2000-5 could carry up to four MICA EM missiles and two MICA IRs. There was also a two-seater version, where the back-seater also had a HUD; these aircraft had the internal cannon deleted.

Dassault found it tough to sell the Mirage 2000-5 abroad initially, since

▷ DASSAULT-BREGUET MIRAGE 2000-5EI

Dassault Mirage 2000-5EI, 2020/EI-20, 499th Tactical Fighter Wing, Republic of China Air Force, Hsinchu air base, Taiwan, 2017.
This aircraft has tail art to commemorate 20 years of Mirage operations with the RoCAF. Taiwan was the first customer for the improved Mirage 2000-5 variant; some export aircraft (like this one) have an arrestor hook installed.

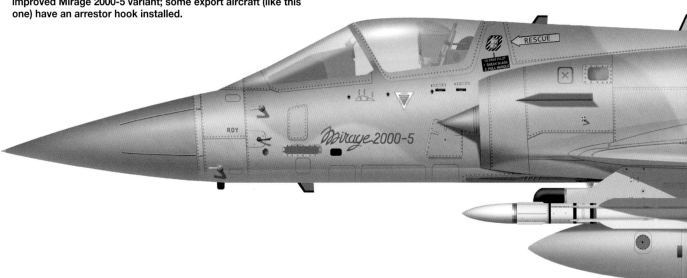

▷ DASSAULT-BREGUET MIRAGE 2000-5F

Dassault Mirage 2000-5F, 2-EJ/43, Escadron de Chasse 1/2 Cigognes, Escadrille SPA 3 'Cigogne de Guynemer', Armée de l'Air (Fighter squadron 1/2, Flight SPA 3, French Air Force), air base 116, Luxeuil-Saint-Sauveur, France, 2017.
With a special paint scheme marking the 100th anniversary of the death of Captain Georges Guynemer, this aircraft carries the inscription 'Vieux Charles' like the aircraft flown by the legendary French pilot.

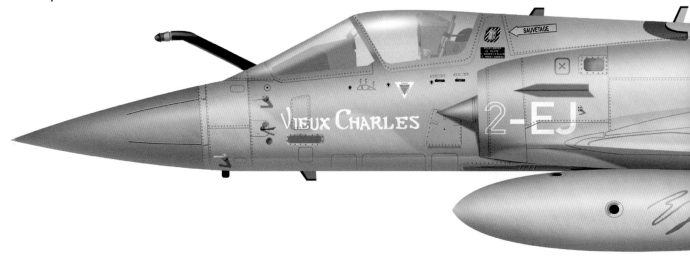

it hadn't been bought by the French government. While declining to buy new airframes, after some lobbying France did agree in 1993 to upgrade 37 of its existing late-production Mirage 2000Cs to 2000-5 standard. These were designated Mirage 2000-5F and entered service in 2000. These aircraft kept their old countermeasures systems and did not receive ICMS 2.

During the Gulf War in 1991, French Mirage 2000Cs provided high-altitude defence for American U-2 reconnaissance aircraft but saw little action. Mirage 2000Ns did, however, see combat during the UN and NATO operations over the former Yugoslavia in the 1990s, with a Mirage 2000N-K2 being shot down by a heat-seeking 9K38 Igla missile over Bosnia on August 30, 1995.

French Air Force Mirage 2000Ds served with international forces over Afghanistan in 2001 and during the French intervention in Mali in 2013.

Since 2014, French Mirage 2000s have flown operations over the Sahel region of Africa against Russian-backed militants, operating from Niamey in Niger. Two Mirage 2000D RMVs were deployed there in March 2023.

▼ DASSAULT-BREGUET MIRAGE 2000EM

Dassault-Breguet Mirage 2000EM, 108/9608, 82nd Tactical Fighter Squadron, 252nd Tactical Fighter Wing, Egyptian Air Force, Ebel el Basur air base, Egypt, 2014.
Egypt was the first export customer for the Mirage 2000, operating a single squadron of the type.

▶ DASSAULT-BREGUET MIRAGE 2000C

Dassault-Breguet Mirage 2000C, 12-YM/115, Escadron de Chasse 1/12 'Cambrésis', Armée de l'Air, (Fighter squadron 1/12, French Air Force), Albacete air base, Spain, 2006.
This was a special paint scheme for the 2006 NATO Tiger Meet.

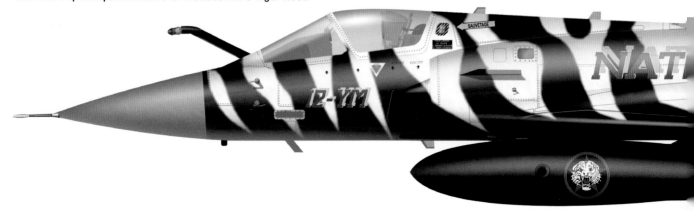

DASSAULT-BREGUET MIRAGE 2000EG

Dassault-Breguet Mirage 2000EG, 239, 332 MPK, Polemikí Aeroporía (332 All-Weather Squadron, Hellenic Air Force), Tanagra air base, Greece, 2014.
This Mirage carries tail-art to commemorate the 25th anniversary of the squadron and is equipped with Exocet anti-ship missiles. Greece also bought the later 2000-5 Mk.2 variant.

All Mirage 2000Ns had been retired by June 2018, having been replaced by Rafales, and the last Mirage 2000Cs were finally retired on June 23, 2022. Sixty-eight 2000Ds and 24 2000-5Fs were still in service at the time of writing.

EGYPT
The first overseas nation to adopt the Mirage 2000 was Egypt, with a one-off order for 16 Mirage 2000EM single-seat fighters and four Mirage 2000BM two-seat trainers placed in December 1981 and deliveries beginning in 1986. A 2000EM crashed on November 30, 1999, 60 miles north of Cairo and the pilot was killed. Nearly 20 years later, in April 2019, a 2000BM crashed with both crew ejecting safely. Today Egypt continues to fly its 18 remaining Mirage 2000s.

INDIA
Following hot on Egypt's heels, India ordered a batch of 26 single-seat Mirage 2000H5s and four two-seater Mirage 2000TH5s in 1982. The '5' was in reference to the engine, since these were fitted with the M53-5, rather than the M53-P2 which wasn't yet ready. Deliveries began in 1985 and the aircraft was given the name 'Vajra' or 'Thunderbolt'. A second batch of ten aircraft followed, this time powered by the M53-P2, and the original 30 aircraft were brought up to the same standard as Mirage 2000Hs and 2000THs.

Six more 2000H single-seaters and three more 2000TH trainers were delivered between 1987 and 1988, giving India a total of 49 Mirage 2000s. Another ten 2000Hs with RDM 7 radar and improved avionics were bought in 2004.

An upgrade programme was started in 2011 to bring all IAF Mirage 2000Hs up to Mirage 2000-5 Mk.2 standard, with the first updated machine being redelivered in 2015. The 2000-5 Mk.2 modification features a Thales RDY-2 radar, Rafale-style computer, Thales Totem 3000 INS with ring-laser gyros and GPS, on-board oxygen generation, ICMS 3 digital countermeasures, datalink, optional SATURN secure radio and updated cockpit displays. It also allows the SCALP cruise missile and MICA missiles to be carried. IAF aircraft receiving the update were redesignated Mirage 2000I and 2000TI.

Indian Mirage 2000s have seen action on several occasions over the years – particularly during border clashes with Pakistan over Kashmir. Twenty Indian Mirage 2000s entered Pakistani airspace on February 26, 2019 and dropped 1,000kg laser-guided bombs on an alleged terrorist training camp in Balakot.

A total of 14 Indian Mirage 2000s have been lost in accidents and due to technical issues between 1987 and 2019. In 2021, India bought 24 ex-French Air Force Mirage 2000s to break for spares.

▼ DASSAULT-BREGUET MIRAGE 2000C

Dassault-Breguet Mirage 2000C (F-2000C), 4940, 1.° Grupo de Defesa Aérea, Força Aérea Brasileira (1st Air Defence Group, Brazilian Air Force), Anápolis air base, Brazil, 2010.
While awaiting the selection of its next fighter, Brazil bought ex-French Air Force Mirage 2000s to provide air defence capability.

▼ DASSAULT-BREGUET MIRAGE 2000-5EDA

Dassault Mirage 2000-5EDA, QA-95, 7th Air Superiority Squadron, 1st Fighter Wing, Qatar Emiri Air Force, Doha air base, Qatar, 2014.
Qatar's Mirage 2000s entered frontline service in 1997 and have since been replaced by Rafales. In 2011 they were used during no-fly enforcement operations over Libya.

▼ DASSAULT-BREGUET MIRAGE 2000-5F

Dassault Mirage 2000-5F, 2-EA, Escadron de Chasse 1/2 Cigognes, Armée de l'Air et de l'Espace (Fighter squadron 1/2, French Air & Space Force), air base 116, Luxeuil – Saint-Sauveur, France, 2019.
A special tail-art was applied to this aircraft to celebrate 20 years of the 2000-5F variant in service. This aircraft also carries both IR and radar-guided variants of the Matra MICA air-to-air missile.

F-2000C
4940

MIRAGE
2000-5

QA95

20ANS
d'excellence

ABU DHABI/UAE

An order for 22 Mirage 2000EAD single-seat fighters, eight unusual reconnaissance-equipped 2000RAD single-seaters and six two-seat 2000DAD trainers was placed by Abu Dhabi in 1983. These were to be fitted with Italian avionics, which delayed their delivery until 1989. While the 2000EAD corresponded to the 2000C and the 2000DAD to the 2000B, the 2000RAD was unique – it carried no internal sensors or cameras but could instead carry one of three reconnaissance pods: the Thales SLAR 2000 radar pod, Dassault's COR2 camera pod or the AA-3-38 HAROLD telescopic long-range optical camera pod, also made by Dassault.

The new aircraft were involved in the Gulf War of 1991 but saw very little action. The UAE then ordered 20 Mirage 2000-9 single-seat fighters and 12 two-seater Mirage 2000-9D aircraft. These came with IMEWS countermeasures systems, the Shehab laser targeting pod and the Naher nav pod, complementing the air-to-ground modes of the RDY-2 radar.

Deliveries of these 32 new-build aircraft started in 2003, with 30 of the UAE's older Mirage 2000s also being upgraded to 2000-9 standard. In 2019, Dassault received a $489.5 million contract to upgrade the fleet further. In April 2022, it was reported that the UAE was offering its entire Mirage 2000 fleet to Morocco and Egypt. However, in August 2022 it was suggested that in fact Greece might be buying the UAE's aircraft instead.

GREECE

The Greek government ordered 36 Mirage 2000EG single-seaters and four Mirage 2000BG two-seat trainers in March 1985 and they were delivered between 1988 and 1989. Under a 1990s modernisation programme, Greek Mirage 2000s received the much improved RDM-3 radar, ICMS 1 DCS and the ability to carry the Super 530D medium-range missile and the AM39 Exocet. These upgraded aircraft were redesignated Mirage 2000EGM/BGM.

An order for 15 new Mirage 2000-5 Mk.2s was placed in August 2000 and ten existing 2000EGMs were upgraded to 2000-5 Mk.2 standard.

During a confrontation on October 8, 1996, a Greek Mirage 2000 reportedly fired an R.550 Magic 2 missile at a Turkish F-16D. Turkey claims that the aircraft was shot down but Greece denies this. In April 2018, a Hellenic Air Force pilot was killed when his Mirage 2000-5 crashed during a mock dogfight with Turkish F-16s. Today Greece continues to operate around 42 Mirage 2000s.

PERU

A dozen Mirage 2000s – ten 2000P single-seaters and a pair of 2000DP two-seaters – were ordered by Peru in 1986. They saw limited action in a border clash with Ecuador in 1995 and from 2009 they received a minor avionics update. All 12 examples are still in service today.

TAIWAN

Sixty Mirage 2000-5s were bought by Taiwan in 1992: 48 2000-5EI single-seaters and 12 2000-5DI two-seat trainers. The first aircraft arrived in May 1997 and the type entered active service in 1998. One crashed during a routine training mission on March 14, 2022, after the pilot noticed a lack of power and ejected safely. Today 54 examples remain in service.

▽ DASSAULT-BREGUET MIRAGE 2000DP

Dassault-Breguet Mirage 2000DP, 195, Escuadrón de Caza 412, Grupo Aéreo N°4, Fuerza Aérea del Perú (412 Fighter Squadron, Air Group No. 4, Peruvian Air Force), Coronel FAP Víctor Maldonado Begazo air base, Arequipa Peru, 2005.
Delivered in 1986, Peruvian Mirage 2000s were involved in the 1995 Cenepa War against Ecuador; this desert colour scheme was the first used by Peruvian Mirages.

▽ DASSAULT-BREGUET MIRAGE 2000P

Dassault-Breguet Mirage 2000P, 062, Escuadrón de Caza 412, Grupo Aéreo N°4, Fuerza Aérea del Perú (412 Fighter Squadron, Air Group No. 4, Peruvian Air Force), Las Palmas air base, Santiago de Surco, Peru, 2014.
Painted in the later all-grey colour scheme, this Mirage's tail-art celebrates the 100th anniversary of the birth of Captain José A. Quiñones Gonzales, hero of the FAP.

QATAR

Nine Mirage 2000-5EDA single-seaters and three Mirage 2000-5DDA trainers were ordered by Qatar in 1994 with deliveries commencing in late 1997. The Qatar Emiri Air Force began to phase them out in 2019 and in November 2021 the whole fleet of 12 was reportedly purchased by private French pilot training contractor ARES.

BRAZIL

Brazil agreed to buy nine Mirage 2000Cs and two Mirage 2000Bs, ex-French Air Force machines, on July 15, 2005, with deliveries taking place between September 2006 and 2008. Known as F-2000 in Brazilian service, they were withdrawn on December 31, 2013, after just over seven years due to high operating costs. Nine of them, eight F-2000Cs and one F-2000B, were reportedly sold to French company Procor in May 2019 for use as aggressors in fighter pilot training.

DASSAULT
RAFALE

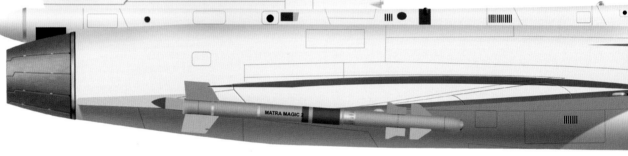

▲ DASSAULT-BREGUET RAFALE A

Dassault-Breguet Rafale A, Salon International de l'Aéronautique et de l'Espace, Le Bourget airport, France, 1989.
The Rafale prototype as it appeared at the Paris Air Show, displaying, on the fin, the number of flights made until then; note the Aéronavale's roundel on the intake. The aircraft still has General Electric F404 engines at this stage, before being equipped with SNECMA M88s.

The 'omnirole' Dassault Rafale is France's primary in-service combat aircraft and is more popular with export customers now, nearly two decades after its introduction, than ever before.

British company British Aerospace (BAe) and German firm Messerschmitt-Bölkow-Blohm (MBB) presented their governments with a combined proposal for a European Combat Aircraft (ECF) in 1979. The goal was to replace various existing types including the Jaguar and Harrier with a single modern high-performance multirole machine.

At the same time, the French Air Force also found itself with an inventory full of different types developed using older technology that were expensive to maintain and were approaching obsolescence – the Mirage III, 5 and F1 fighters, the SEPECAT Jaguar strike aircraft and the Mirage IV bomber. It was clear that the Aéronavale's Étendards, Super Étendards and Vought F-8s would need to be replaced too.

While it was a modern multirole fighter, even the Mirage 2000 was based on designs for a relatively simple fighter for export and the aircraft was not suitable for naval use. Consequently the Air Force issued a requirement for an Avion de Combat Tactique (ACT/Tactical Combat Aircraft), with the Aéronavale seeking an Avion de Combat Marine (ACM/Naval Combat Aircraft) in parallel.

Since there were many areas overlap between the two, it was agreed to combine the ACT and ACM into a single requirement – ACX/Avion de Combat Experimental. Dassault drafted a proposal for this requirement then joined the ECF programme and merged its ACX design with those of BAe and MBB.

At this point, the French insisted that Dassault should be appointed project leader, with design authority, whereas the other partners preferred a more cooperative approach. As such, Dassault left ECF in 1981. BAe and MBB, who had previously worked together on Tornado, then joined Italian Aeritalia to launch the Agile Combat Aircraft (ACA) study programme in April 1982 and funding was secured for two prototypes, eventually reduced to just one.

DASSAULT RAFALE C

Dassault Rafale C 01, Salon International de l'Aéronautique et de l'Espace, Le Bourget airport, France, 1993.
The first Rafale C was painted in this all-black colour scheme to emphasize its stealth capabilities; it displays the emblems of several French Air Force escadrilles on the front lower fuselage.

▽ DASSAULT RAFALE C

Dassault Rafale C, 4-GL/133, Escadron de Transformation Rafale 3/4 Aquitaine, SPA 160 'Diable Rouge', Armée de l'Air (Rafale Conversion Squadron 3/4, Flight 160, French Air Force), Salon-de-Provence Air Show, France, 2017.
The solo Rafale display aircraft for the 2017 season is shown here as it appeared at the Salon-de-Provence air show; ETR 3/4 is the Rafale operational conversion unit of the French Air Force.

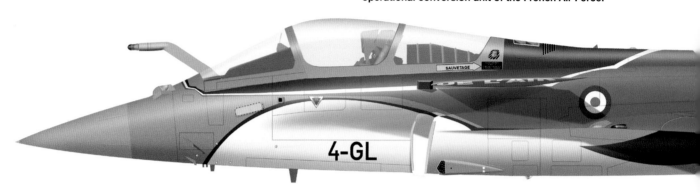

▽ DASSAULT RAFALE M

Dassault Rafale M, 37, Flotille 11F Hippocampe, Aeronavale, Marine Nationale (Squadron 11F, Naval Air Arm, French Navy), Landivisiau naval air base, 2019.
Several aircraft received special paint schemes for the centenary of Flotille 11F, each representing an aircraft flown previously by the unit; this one represents the Grumman F6F-5 Hellcat. The aircraft carries a buddy refuelling pod.

▽ DASSAULT RAFALE M

Dassault Rafale M, 5, Flotille 12F Canard fusilier-marin, Aeronavale, Marine Nationale (Squadron 12F, Naval Air Arm, French Navy), Landivisiau naval air base, France, 2018.
The fin art on this Rafale M commemorates the 70th anniversary of Flotille 12F; the aircraft carries both IR and radar-guided variants of the Matra MICA air-to-air missile and the Thales Damocles pod.

The following year, yet another programme was begun – Future European Fighter Aircraft (FEFA) – with France and Spain both joining Britain, German and Italy. However, the French once again tried to claim design authority over the project. Consequently, Britain and German left to pursue their own European Fighter Aircraft (EFA) programme in 1984, with Italy and Spain joining them in 1985. This would become the Eurofighter Typhoon.

Dassault was left to develop its ACX aircraft alone, giving it the name Rafale, meaning 'squall' or 'gust of wind'. At the same time SNECMA was developing a new afterburning bypass turbojet designated M88. Construction of a Rafale A technology demonstrator started in March 1984 and was completed on December 14, 1985.

The result was a curvy, sleek-looking canard delta aircraft powered by a pair of General Electric F404-GE-400 afterburning turbofans, as used in the F/A-18, since the M88 was not yet ready. It first flew on July 4, 1986, piloted by Guy Mitaux-Maurouard, and made its public debut that September. The French government eventually ordered the type into production in April 1988 with three variants envisioned: the single-seat Rafale C, two-seat Rafale B and single-seat naval Rafale M, following the now-familiar French fighter naming convention of 'Chasseur', 'Biplace' and 'Marine' respectively.

The Aéronavale would later also specify its own two-seater – the Rafale BM – but this was cancelled in 2004.

The Rafale C 01 prototype first flew in May 1991, followed by the first Rafale M 01 prototype in December 1991 and the B 01 in April 1993. That same month, the M 01 made its first deck landing on the French carrier *Foch*.

Slightly smaller than the Rafale A prototype and made using composite materials, the Rafale C is powered by two M88-2 bypass turbojets with fixed inlets. The design incorporates some semi-stealth features such as radar absorbing materials and a reduced radar cross section. It has a low-mounted main wing with all-moving high-mounted canards just behind the cockpit, a brake chute in a fairing below the tailfin and a removeable refuelling probe on the upper right side of the nose. The nose gear has two wheels and the main gear has one each, all retracting forwards.

A single 30mm GIAT 791B cannon is housed in the right engine duct and 14 pylons, including wingtip rails for AAMs, can be used to carry up to 9,500kg of stores. Options include everything from MICA IRs and EMs to Meteor BVRAAMs, Paveway bombs, SCALP cruise missiles, the Thales Damocles targeting pod, Thales Reco NG reconnaissance pod, AASM guided bombs and even the ASMPA nuclear standoff missile. The two inner pylons on each wing and the rear

▽ DASSAULT RAFALE B

Dassault Rafale B, 4-HT/323, Escadron de Chasse 1/4 Gascogne, Escadrille BR 66 – 'Faucon égyptien', Armée de l'Air (Fighter Squadron 1/4, Flight BR 66, French Air Force), Jordan, 2015.
This Rafale B is shown as it appeared during Operátion Chammal against Daesh forces in Syria; it carries the SCALP-EG cruise missile and displays mission markings on its nose.

▽ DASSAULT RAFALE B

Dassault Rafale B, Western Air Command, Fighter Wing, United Arab Emirates Air Force and Air Defence, Al Dhafra Air Base, Abu Dhabi, United Arab Emirates, 2028.
UAE signed a deal in 2021 for the delivery of 80 Rafales; this is how one might look in UAEAF&AD service. This aircraft carries GBU-49 laser-guided bombs and the Thales Damocles pod.

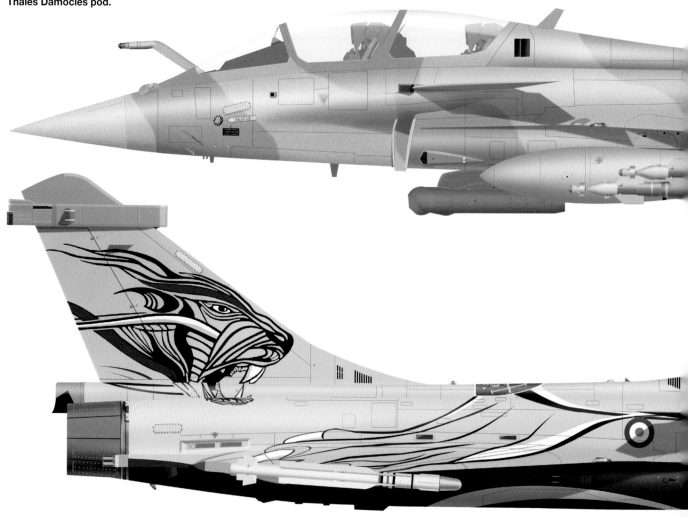

centreline pylon can be used to carry external tanks.

Inside the Rafale C's cockpit is a Martin-Baker Mk16F ejection seat, an oxygen generation system, HOTAS controls, HUD, direct voice input capability, multifunction displays and SAGEM Gerfaut helmet-mounted sight. Avionics include RBE2 multimode radar, Thales/SAGEM optical sensor suite, IRST infrared search and track unit, TV/laser rangefinder, ring-laser gyro nav system with GPS, secure radio system, tactical datalink and Thales/Matra BAE Dynamics SPECTRA digital countermeasures. The latter, which includes four chaff/flare dispensers alongside active jammers and warning sensors, is built into the airframe and therefore takes up no stores space.

The Rafale B two-seater retains the C's operational equipment and therefore its operational capability, sacrificing only internal fuel capacity to provide room for the back-seater. The Rafale M was externally very similar to the C but with an arrestor hook under the tail and with only 13 stores pylons – the forward centreline position being deleted to provide space for longer nose gear. The C and B also have an arrestor hook but it is less prominent.

Internally, the M has a strengthened airframe and main gear, powered pilot boarding ladder, carrier microwave landing system and Telemir inertial nav system. All this makes the Rafale M 500kg heavier than the Rafale C.

The first Rafale delivery to the French Air Force was a two-seat Rafale B in December 2000 and the first Rafale Ms were delivered to the Aéronavale in December 2001. The type formally entered service with the Aéronavale in 2004 and with the French Air Force in 2006.

The earliest Rafales were built to F1 standard, which gave them only the avionics they needed for air-to-air combat – making them still good enough to replace the Aéronavale's F-8s. In fact, the earliest Rafale Ms were delivered below F1 standard as 'LF1' with old mission computers and without cannon. These were later updated to F1 standard.

F2 standard introduced ground-attack capability, allowing the Rafale to carry and use LGBs and the SCALP cruise missile as well as its single built-in cannon. It also allowed the aircraft to carry MICA IRs in place of the old Magic missile and support for a buddy tanker pack was included.

F3 standard included everything else that the Rafale was supposed to have – additional modes for the RBE2 radar, AASM capability, nuclear strike with the ASMPA, Exocet or ANF carriage and the Reco NG pod. This was the point at which DVI and other advanced cockpit features were added. The first F3 standard aircraft were delivered in 2009 and all existing Rafales were then upgraded to the same standard.

The next upgrade was to F3-R standard, which included the vastly improved RBE2-AA Active Electronically

DASSAULT RAFALE C

Dassault Rafale C, 113-HJ, Escadron de Chasse 1/7 'Provence', Armée de l'Air (Fighter Squadron 1/7, French Air Force), Ørland air base, Norway, 2013. A special paint scheme for the 2013 NATO Tiger Meet.

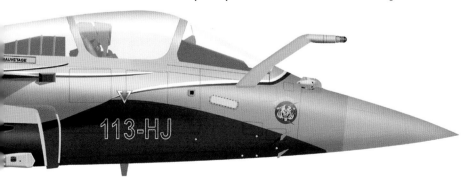

Scanned Array (AESA) radar unit. F3-R also included the FSO-IT optical-infrared forward-looking sensor system, enhanced datalink, improvements to the SPECTRA system and a new Targeting Long Range identification Optronics System (TALIOS) pod starting in 2018. The first F3-R aircraft were evaluated from late 2013 and the variant entered service in 2019.

F4 standard was unveiled in 2017 and an initial prototype flew in 2021. This includes improvements to the RBE2-AA, the Reco NG pod and the TALIOS pod, improved helmet-mounted display with satellite link, support for the MICA NG missile, and a new engine control unit and diagnostics system. The first F4.1

▼ DASSAULT RAFALE DM

Dassault Rafale DM, DM-01/9201, 203rd Tactical Fighter Wing, 34th Tactical Fighter Squadron 'Wild Wolves', Egyptian Air Force, Gebel El Basur Air Base Egypt, 2018. Egypt was the earliest export customer for the Rafale, receiving its first aircraft in 2017 and putting them into action in Libya that same year; this aircraft carries AASM (Armement Air-Sol Modulaire) Hammer guided bombs.

▼ DASSAULT RAFALE C

Dassault Rafale, 191. eskadrila lovačkih aviona, Hrvatsko ratno zrakoplovstvo (191st fighter squadron, Croatian Air Force), 91st air force base, Pleso, Croatia, 2027.
A contract for the supply of Rafales to the HRZ was signed in November 2021; this is a speculative image of how these aircraft might look, replicating the colour scheme seen on MiG-21s in Croatian service.

aircraft was delivered to the French Air Warfare Centre for testing on March 2, 2023.

At the time of writing, the French Air and Space Force (the new name for the French Air Force as of 2020) was still expecting to acquire a total of 212 Rafales, with about 40% of them being two-seaters. A total of 102 had been delivered by December 31, 2018, with another 44 having gone to the Aéronavale – a total of 146 excluding prototypes – when deliveries ground to a halt for budgetary reasons. They resumed on December 29, 2022.

From the spring of 2007, a number of Rafales were involved in supporting NATO troops against Taliban forces in Afghanistan. The first aircraft deployed were F2s, followed by some F3 machines in 2010. Meanwhile, in September 2009, two Aéronavale Rafale Ms crashed into the Mediterranean with only one pilot known to have ejected safely.

Rafales flew NATO combat missions during the Libyan revolution in 2011 and during the French intervention in Mali against Islamist insurgents in 2013. This expanded into attacks on Islamists in the Central African Republic and Nigeria, then against insurgents in Iraq and Syria from 2014. Intensive strikes were made on Islamic State forces after the terror attacks in Paris on November 13/14, 2015. During 2019, one of the Rafales being flown against IS forces was seen with a drone 'kill mark' – suggesting that this was the Rafale's first air-to-air kill.

▷ DASSAULT RAFALE B

DASSAULT RAFALE M
Dassault Rafale M, 46, Flotille 17F Balbuzard, Aeronavale, Marine Nationale (Squadron 17F, Naval Air Arm, French Navy), *Charles de Gaule* aircraft carrier, 2024.
The Aéronavale's Rafales also have a nuclear strike role, carrying the ASMP cruise missile. This aircraft also carries Matra MICA and MBDA Meteor missiles.

DASSAULT RAFALE B

Dassault Rafale B, 4-FR/351, Escadron de Chasse 2/4 La Fayette, Forces Aerienes Strategiques, Armée de l'Air et de l'Espace (Fighter Squadron 2/4, Strategic Air Forces, French Air & Space Force), air base 113, Saint-Dizier – Robinson, France, 2019.
French Rafales can carry the ASMP-A cruise missile for nuclear strike missions should the need arise.

DASSAULT RAFALE EH

Dassault Rafale EH, BS-010, No. 101 Squadron 'Falcons', Indian Air Force, Hasimara Air Force Station, India, 2023. The first IAF Rafale squadron was formed in 2021, with both single and two-seater aircraft; this example carries Matra MICA and MBDA Meteor air-to-air missiles.

▽ DASSAULT RAFALE C

Dassault Rafale C, Tentara Nasional Indonesia-Angkatan Udara (Indonesian Air Force), Indonesia, 2030.
Indonesia signed a letter of intent to buy Rafales in 2021 and this a speculative colour scheme. The aircraft carries the Exocet anti-ship missile.

▽ DASSAULT RAFALE EQ

Dassault Rafale EQ, QA-232, Al Adiyat Fighter Squadron, Qatar Emiri Air Force, Dukhan/ Tamim air base, Qatar, 2022.
This Rafale carries an air-to-air weapons load of Matra MICA AAMs.

DASSAULT RAFALE B

Dassault Rafale B, 401, 332 MPK, Polemikí Aeroporía (332 All-Weather Squadron, Hellenic Air Force), Tanagra air base, Greece, 2023.
This was the first Rafale delivered to the Hellenic Air force in 2021; it was part of a group of former French Air Force aircraft which, together with newly built examples, will be delivered to Greece.

EGYPT

The first foreign order for Rafales was finalised by Egypt in February 2015 and included 24 F3-R standard aircraft – 16 Rafale DM two-seaters and eight Rafale EM single-seaters. Deliveries took place between 2015 and 2019, the type then entering active service with the Egyptian Air Force in 2018. A second order, for another 30, was placed in September 2021.

QATAR

A memorandum of understanding for the supply of 24 Rafales was signed by Qatar in May 2015, comprising 18 single-seat Rafale EQs and six two-seat Rafale DQs. Another dozen aircraft were added to the deal in December 2017 for a total of 36, with Qatar retaining an option to purchase another 36 on top of that. The first Rafale built for Qatar, a DQ made its initial flight in France on June 28, 2016, and the first EQ flew on March

27, 2017. The first 15 aircraft – 12 EQs and three DQs – were delivered in 2019.

INDIA
The Indian government indicated an intention to purchase 36 Rafales in April 2015 but the deal did not go through until September 2016. It included 28 Rafale EH single-seaters and eight Rafale DH two-seaters. The first 35 aircraft were delivered within 67 months – from September 2019 to April 2022, with the 36th aircraft initially being retained in France before finally being delivered in December 2022. It was reported in March 2023 that India was seeking to buy 26 new Rafale M aircraft, which would bring the country's total to 62.

GREECE
The Greek government signed a deal for 18 Rafales on January 2021 – 12 used and six new. The first six examples, four Rafale EG single seaters and two Rafale ED two-seaters, being delivered a year later in January 2022. An additional six aircraft were then ordered in March 2022 for a total of 24.

CROATIA
Croatia agreed to buy 12 ex-French Air Force Rafales in November 2021, with France itself then buying a dozen new examples from Dassault to replace them. The first six are due for delivery to Croatia in 2024 with the remaining six to be supplied in 2025.

INDONESIA & UAE
February 2022 saw Indonesia purchasing 42 Rafales, with the first six to be delivered by 2026, while the United Arab Emirates signed a deal in December 2021 to buy a record 80 examples, all of them built to the latest F4 standard. Deliveries to the UAE are set to take place from 2026 to 2031.

▼ FCAS
A not-so-distant future sight? This is a possible configuration for the Future Combat Air System (FCAS), seen here controlling combat drones.